"The book of Daniel has an important message for Christians today who live in cultures that are toxic to their faith. Daniel himself lived in such a culture and shows how faith can thrive even when threatened by the world around us. The book of Daniel also reminds us again and again that in spite of difficulties, God is in control and will have the final victory. Barbara M. Leung Lai brings her considerable knowledge and clear insight into her concise yet substantial presentation of the book. I recommend *Glimpsing the Mystery* to all who not only want to understand the book of Daniel better, but also have it transform their lives and faith."

> –Tremper Longman III, Robert H. Gundry Professor of Biblical Studies, Westmont College

"For many, the Book of Daniel seems largely enigmatic and incomprehensible. In this volume, Dr. Barbara Leung Lai takes this challenging book and ably opens it up for the contemporary reader. Through an analysis of the book's historical context, literary forms, theological emphases, and most especially of the character of Daniel as presented in the book, she leads her readers to an understanding of how they too can appropriate the message of Daniel in their own experiential context. Her discussion of the book's portrait of both the public and private life of Daniel is especially compelling, as are her own personal reflections on how she has wrestled with the book's theological message in her own experience. The discussion and study questions at the end of each chapter make the book an excellent resource for students and group Bible studies. Dr. Leung Lai helps her readers grasp the core values of the book, and their significance for life today."

> –John Kessler, professor of Old Testament and chair of biblical studies, Tyndale Seminary, Toronto

"A lucid treatise on the profound yet enigmatic book of Daniel, leading readers soaring high to a panoramic view of the sovereignty of God in human history, coming down deep into the inner world of Daniel the person and the Jewish community, and experiencing its messages from the past in today's perplexed world."

–Rev. Terence Lau, Ph.D., minister-at-large, Christian and Missionary Alliance in Canada

GLIMPSING THE MYSTERY

THE BOOK OF DANIEL

GLIMPSING THE MYSTERY

THE BOOK OF DANIEL

TRANSFORMATIVE WORD

BARBARA M. LEUNG LAI

Edited by Craig G. Bartholomew

LEXHAM PRESS

Glimpsing the Mystery: The Book of Daniel

Copyright 2016 Barbara Leung Lai

Lexham Press, 1313 Commercial St., Bellingham, WA 98225
LexhamPress.com

Print ISBN 9781577997740
Digital ISBN 9781577997757

Lexham Editorial: Sarah Awa, Amy Balogh, Elliot Ritzema,
    Abby Salinger, Abigail Stocker
Cover Design: Bryan Hintz
Back Cover Design: Liz Donovan
Typesetting: ProjectLuz.com

To the Leung Sisters: Christine, Grace, Gladys
Family, Friends, Fellow Pilgrims

TABLE OF CONTENTS

INTRODUCTION

On the evening of September 11, 2001, I began teaching a course on Daniel and apocalyptic literature. Students were stunned by the tragic events still unfolding through the afternoon hours into the evening. A student whose husband, daughter, and son-in-law were working in the World Trade Center was sitting in the corner of the room. When asked, she refused to go home and wait for phone calls. Instead, she chose to stay with the class through those agonizing hours. (She would later learn that her immediate family all survived, but she lost her niece in the tragedy.) It was more than a coincidence that I had adopted my course's subtitle from the theme identified by Tremper Longman III in his commentary on Daniel: "In spite of present appearances, God is in control."[1]

The book of Daniel was written at a time of great national peril to encourage Jews by reminding them that the sovereign God is still in control, despite their current situation. This timeless message has appealed to generations of saints—from the exilic community of the sixth century BC to the faith communities of today. It spoke to the rise and fall of kings and empires in Daniel's time, and it speaks to the turbulent and chaotic situations on the current world scene. Wars and conflicts among nations, global catastrophes that are beyond human control, and the magnitude and intensity of senseless human suffering—all these have the potential to shake our faith to its core. We share the same genuine need as Daniel (12:6), and with him as well as the prophets and psalmists we ask: "How long?" (Pss 80:4; 82:2).

Engaging the Book of Daniel "In Times Like This"

I am Chinese-Canadian, with a ministry primarily among the Chinese faith communities in the Toronto metro area. In my faith community, we have strategically used the book of Daniel to help members come to terms with the realities of the new world after the tragedy of September 11, 2001. Studying this profoundly pastoral book, people often find comfort and strength in applying Daniel's message to their own contexts. The book has proven meaningful when read as a survival manual for immigrant families, for those who are under hostile rule, or for those who are facing extreme trials of faith.[2]

I am also in the prime of my life, with a ministry among my privileged peers—well-educated, middle-class professionals, Chinese and non-Chinese prime-timers. Within this context, one reality persistently disturbs the community: Our collective Canadian culture, our professional lives, and our social and economic status cannot adequately provide answers to the senselessness and absurdity of human suffering. As in the case of Daniel's community in captivity, we look to the future with a high degree of uncertainty but glimpses of hope. In our view of God, we need to include the idea that God is the one who reveals and yet, by his sovereignty, leaves us in a certain degree of suspense about end-time mysteries.

As we read Daniel, we are reminded that a great deal is happening "underwater," though oftentimes we see only ripples. God's greatness and sovereignty can be experienced through everyday stories in our lives but also go beyond them. This understanding is, potentially, a transformative path leading to enduring faith and perseverance.

> God's greatness and sovereignty can be experienced through everyday stories in our lives but also go beyond them.

Toward the end of the book, after beholding extraordinary visions of God and going through an exotic visionary experience, Daniel is given a calming assurance: "But you, Daniel, go on to the end; for you shall rest and stand in your lot at the end of the days" (12:13, my translation). The book ends suddenly and unexpectedly with a serene but assuring hope. As Longman has stated, "The book of Daniel masterfully demonstrates God's sovereignty over his people's past, present, and future. God's sovereignty infuses his people with confidence and hope in the midst of a difficult world."[3] In our own faith journeys, perhaps an assuring hope is enough—in spite of current appearances.

The Book and Its Background

The twelve chapters of Daniel are set within a historical framework that extends over three empires—

Babylonian, Median-Persian, and Greek—and four kings: the Babylonian kings Nebuchadnezzar and Belshazzar, the Median king Darius, and the Persian king Cyrus the Great. It is written in two distinct biblical genres: court tales (Dan 1–6) and apocalyptic literature (Dan 7–12). Court tales are stories set within a royal court and usually feature an underling character who is put in precarious positions by the king, only to be delivered by God (compare the story of Joseph in Genesis 39–41). "Apocalyptic" is a genre of writing that particularly focuses on revealing future actions and divine judgment in symbolic terms. The designation "apocalyptic" comes from the Greek word *apokalypsis*, which means "revelation, unveiling." The genre is especially concerned with unveiling details about the last things. Daniel is the most characteristically apocalyptic book in the Old Testament; the genre remained popular into the early Christian era (AD 200).

According to Daniel 1:1–2, 21; 6:28; and 10:1, the book was written in the sixth century BC—from the exile that occurred in the third year of King Jehoiakim (1:1; 605 BC) to the latest reference in the fourth vision given to Daniel, "in the third year of Cyrus king of Persia" (10:1; 536 BC). These references to particular dates and figures at the beginning of each of the court tales (1:1–2; 2:1; 3:1; 4:4; 5:1; 6:1) and more precisely at the beginning of each of the four visions (7:1; 8:1; 9:1; 10:1) are characteristic of the book of Daniel. If the reader pays close attention to the historical references that frame the court tales, a consistent pattern emerges: Each chapter begins with a concrete historical setting (1:1–2; 2:1; 3:1–2; 4:4–5; 5:1–3; 6:1–3) and ends with an appraisal of Daniel's (and his friends') status as it is continuously elevated by the kings he serves (1:18–21; 2:47–49; 3:30; 5:17–18; 6:28).[4]

TIMELINE OF EVENTS IN THE BOOK OF DANIEL

Supported by ancient Near Eastern sources, the historical landscape plays an important role in understanding the book as well as the setting of its first audience: Jews living in exile in Babylon in the sixth century BC. The rise and fall of kings and empires, in fairly quick succession, characterizes the turbulent world context of that time. Daniel 1 begins with Babylon's rise as a world power following its defeat of the Assyrian Empire at the Battle of Nineveh (612 BC). When Nebuchadnezzar II took the throne in 605 BC, Babylon began its ascent to the height of its power, only to decline soon after his death in 562 BC. Another power, Media-Persia, arose next; the Persian king Cyrus the Great took the capital city of Babylon in 539 BC. As reflected in the stories of chapters 1–6, Daniel, his three friends (Shadrach, Meshach, and Abednego), and the Jewish community in captivity had to endure the hostile ruling of these powerful empires, the most extreme of which was Babylon.

The main characters in the court tales are Daniel and his friends, who interact with three foreign kings—Nebuchadnezzar and Belshazzar of Babylon, and Darius of Persia. Daniel takes center stage in the apocalyptic section of the book (Dan 7–12). The last six chapters are written in the first-person voice of Daniel and presented as Daniel's authentic, first-hand vision reports. These chapters include both his visions and their interpretation revealed by angelic beings to Daniel. Through this first-person voice, the author of Daniel invites all readers to engage in his visionary experiences and to take his accounts at face value (for instance, 7:15, 28; 8:27).[5] The book is also written in two languages: 2:4b–7:28 in Aramaic, and the rest in Hebrew.[6]

Date and Author

The dating and authorship of Daniel are debated, with the two most popular options being the sixth or second century BC. Three factors need to be considered:

1. Chapters 1–6 and, to some extent, 7–9 describe things that occurred in the sixth century BC, though the book itself doesn't directly claim a sixth-century date of composition.

2. Writing under the name of a better-known person (a pseudonym—in this case, "Daniel") was a common writing convention in the ancient Near East, especially during the period of Greek, or Hellenistic, rule (323–148 BC). In light of this, we, as readers, should ask: If someone other than the sixth-century Daniel wrote or composed the book, why is the emphatic,

self-referential "I, Daniel" included (7:15, 28; 8:27; 10:2, 7; 12:5) in the first-person, visionary section of the book (Dan 7–12)? How would the original audience have understood and been impacted by it?

3. Reading the text straightforwardly, the vision in chapter 8 extends the scope of the visions to the Greek Empire (especially 8:21, which directly references Greece: "The shaggy goat is the king of Greece, and the large horn between its eyes is the first king").

But ultimately—whether the author's standpoint is from the sixth or second century BC—it makes surprisingly little difference when interpreting the book of Daniel.[7] Though we won't go into a detailed defense of a sixth-century date or Danielic authorship here, we can reach two conclusions from the factors above.

1. While writing under an assumed name was a popular convention in the ancient Near East, the emphatic, self-referential "I, Daniel" is unique among the first-person texts of the Old Testament. (Compare the "I"-voice of the preacher in Ecclesiastes and the four portions of the Nehemiah memoir in Nehemiah [Neh 1:1b–2:20; 4:1–7:73; 12:27–43; 13:1–31]). This uniqueness should be taken into account when determining the authenticity of the sixth-century Daniel behind the "I"-voice.

2. The view that God could reveal to a sixth-century author events that would come to pass in the second century (for example, the direct reference to Greek rule in 8:21), *or* that a

second-century author/composer could record events that were disclosed by God to Daniel back in the sixth century, would each affirm that God is in control throughout human history and beyond (especially chapters 10–12). A parallel example: If we understand the "I"-voice that occurs sporadically throughout the book of Isaiah to be the first-person voice of the eighth-century prophet Isaiah (Isa 5:3, 13; 6:1; 8:1–4; 15:5; 16:4, 9, 11; 21:2–4, 6, 10; 22:4–5, 14; 24:16; 25:1; 26:9, 20; 40:6; 49:1–5; 50:4–9; 61:10; 63:7), then the mentions of Cyrus' name in 44:28 and 45:1 is another powerful witness to a God who reveals future events to the eighth-century audience, because the Persian king Cyrus was born about two centuries *after* the passage was written.

Arrangement of Chapters

As noted previously, one of the characteristics of the book is that the six court tales and the four visions are all prefaced by a precise historical reference (see 1:1–2; 2:1; 3:1; 4:1; 5:1; 6:1; 7:1; 8:1; 9:1; 10:1). However, the chapters are not arranged in chronological order—which highlights the connection between the earthly witnesses in the daily life of the court and the anticipation of God's eternal sovereignty over all evil powers, as revealed through the heavenly visions.

The visions in chapters 7 and 8 occur during the reign of Belshazzar, who reigned as coregent over Babylon with his father Nabonidus (who reigned 556–539 BC). These visions take place before the events of chapter 5. Chapters 6 and 9 take place during

OUTLINE

Six Court Tales (Dan 1–6)
  a. Daniel and His Three Friends in Nebuchadnezzar's Court (Dan 1)
  b. Daniel as Wise Man (Dan 2)
  c. God Saves the Three Friends from the Blazing Furnace (Dan 3)
  d. Nebuchadnezzar's Dream of a Tree and Its Interpretation (Dan 4)
  e. The Writing on the Wall and Its Interpretation (Dan 5)
  f. Daniel in the Lions' Den (Dan 6)

Four Visions (Dan 7–12)
  a. The Vision of the Four Beasts (Dan 7)
  b. The Ram and the Goat (Dan 8)
  c. Daniel's Prayer of Repentance and the Prophecy of the Seventy "Sevens" (Dan 9)
  d. The Vision of a Heavenly Messenger and the Revelation of the Scope and End of History (Dan 10–12)

the reign of Darius the Mede, while the last vision (chs. 10–12) occurs during the reign of Cyrus. The significance of this arrangement is twofold. First, it provides a smooth transition from God's intervention in earthly events through protecting and preserving the life of Daniel and his friends under the reign of the three foreign kings (chs. 1–6) to the mystery of God unfolded in the more sophisticated, heavenly realm presented in chapters 7–12.

Second, this transition is seamless: The community in captivity witnesses God's miraculous work on earth while, at the same time, the heavenly secrets of the sovereign and triumphant God are communicated to Daniel through visions. When told as first-person

RULERS IN THE BOOK OF DANIEL

Ruler	Chapters Present
Nebuchadnezzar	Daniel 1–4
Belshazzar	Daniel 5; 7–8
Darius the Mede	Daniel 6; 9; 11–12
Cyrus the Great	Daniel 6:28; 10

reports, chapters 7–12 are meant to favorably present the recountings as reliable, firsthand accounts.

Case in point: In chapter 8, Daniel is given a vision of the rage between a "ram and a goat" (with the ram as a symbol of the Median and Persian kings/kingdom, 8:19-20; and the goat as the king/kingdom of Greece, 8:21). From the perspective of the sixth-century exilic community (the book's original audience), these historically specific aspects of the vision wouldn't be realized for at least another few centuries. Daniel was so appalled by the vision that he lay ill for several days. Yet he still had to attend to the king's business in the court of Belshazzar (8:1, 27). Daniel's earthly reaction and God's heavenly revelation blend seamlessly together within the same timeframe—the one set by the text of chapter 8.

How to Read the Book

Three reading strategies may be applied to the book of Daniel. First, as Old Testament apocalyptic literature, Daniel may be interpreted according to the guidelines for interpreting apocalyptic literature.[8] We'll talk about these in more detail at relevant moments in the discussion to come.

Second, Daniel can also be read as prophetic liter-ature. Biblical prophecy contains both "forth-telling" (proclamation-making) and "fore-telling" (predic-tion-making) elements. In the case of Daniel, the forth-telling passages are Daniel's interpretations of royal dreams (chs. 2, 4, 5) and the explanations of Daniel's visions by angelic beings (chs. 7–12). Chapter 5 demonstrates the shortest time frame between a fore-telling prophecy and its fulfillment (immediately that night in 5:30–31). Daniel 4:28–34 is another example of the fulfillment of a fore-telling prophecy as "forth-told" (proclaimed) by Daniel through his interpretation of King Nebuchadnezzar's dream (vv. 24–27).

Third, chapters 1–6 could be read as a form of wisdom literature. The idea of wisdom in the Old Testament is rooted in the "two-way doctrine" or "blessing and cursing" as spelled out in Proverbs 3:33 ("The Lord's curse is on the house of the wicked, but he blesses the home of the righteous") and Deuteronomy 11:26–28 (see also Deut 28). The first half of the book could be read from a perspective that emphasizes God's protection of and enabling power on Daniel and his three friends as rewards for their piety and fidelity before him.

Major Theological Themes

One overarching theme of the book of Daniel is the sovereignty of God, as exhibited both on the earthly scene and in the heavenly realm. This emerges from both of the two distinct portions of the book: the court tales (chs. 1–6) and apocalyptic visions (chs. 7–12). God is in control amidst the evil powers of the world, and he is triumphant over the cosmic heavenly conflicts.

A second theological theme throughout the book is the idea that God is the revealer of mysteries. He is truly an "apocalyptic" (revealing) God. At the same time, while God reveals mysteries, he also leaves us in suspense regarding heavenly secrets.

> God is in control amidst the evil powers of the world, and he is triumphant over the cosmic heavenly conflicts.

While these themes run throughout the book, the search for a single theological center of the book should not delimit its significance for the faith community today. As we walk the interpretive path of Daniel's twelve chapters, we will uncover other theological themes brought up by the book's multifaceted view of God and the inner life and probing spirit of Daniel. As we move from an approach that tries to find a single, central theme to a more self-engaged way of reading the book, we will find that reading Daniel can be an ever-enriching and meaning-expanding experience for readers today.

SUGGESTED READING

- ☐ Daniel 1
- ☐ 2 Chronicles 36:15–23
- ☐ Ezra 1
- ☐ Isaiah 44:24–28

Reflection

What does it take for you to feel engaged in reading Daniel?

_____

_____

_____

What is chaotic and crazy about your own life right now? In what ways can we draw on our faith to embrace the realities of life in the twenty-first century?

_____

_____

_____

_____

Reflect on the following quote from John Goldingay, which was referenced in this chapter: "Whether the visions are actual prophecy or quasi-prophecy [i.e., prophecy written after the events], written by Daniel or someone else, in the sixth century BC, the second, or somewhere in between, makes surprisingly little difference to the book's interpretation." Do you agree or disagree? Why or why not?

_____

_____

_____

THE SOVEREIGNTY OF GOD ON THE EARTHLY SCENE

The book of Daniel contains some of the best-known stories in the Old Testament. They include Daniel's interpretation of Nebuchadnezzar's dreams (Dan 2) and the "writing on the wall" (Dan 5); the courageous counter-Babylonian resistance of Daniel's three friends—Shadrach, Meshach, and Abednego—and God's rescue of them from the burning furnace (Dan 3); as well as Daniel's miraculous deliverance from the lions' den (Dan 6).

These are highly dramatic stories of faith and salvation that appeal to children and adults alike. Like biblical interpretation more generally, interpreting these stories is neither a science nor an art—it's both. This means that readers' engagement with the book and its stories is very important.

Two key insights about Hebrew narrative can help us understand these court tales' overall purpose. First, the *way* a story is told is just as, if not *more*, important than *what* is told. Second, biblical authors often use repetition as a technique to highlight importance.[1]

These two insights together provide clues as to the point of view of the narrator (that is, the storyteller) and therefore help us understand the overarching message of the first six chapters of the book.

The major theme of this collection of court tales (chs. 1–6) is the sovereignty of God. Through the interplay between the orders and deeds of the foreign kings on the one hand and the courage and wisdom of Daniel and his three friends on the other, the narrator of these stories seems to ask, "Who is the supreme sovereign"?[2] The question is answered in dramatic ways, often by contrasting an earthly king with the sovereign God, or comparing the wise men of foreign courts (astrologists, diviners, etc.) with the noble servant Daniel. In reading these six court tales as a "survival manual," Shane Kirkpatrick[3] suggests that focusing on God's hand in the story of the Jewish people in captivity underscores the book's central message—that in spite of how things seem from the vantage point of the community, the sovereign God is still in control.

Scholar David M. Valeta adds that chapters 1–6 may be read as "resistance literature" against hostile regimes and control—biblical characters often creatively use satire and humor in order to resist the harsh orders and demands of earthly kings.[4] For example, King Darius is portrayed as weak, manipulated by his own officials (6:8–20). This trait is highlighted by Daniel's portrayal as confident and calm (8:10, 21–23). Similarly, David S. Russell draws four connections between the techniques common in modern political cartoons and those in apocalyptic literature—in our case, the first-person vision reports of Daniel:[5]

1. They give expression to what they want to say in exaggerated form, using striking visuals or literary imagery.

2. They make ample use of traditional and stereo-typed imagery in which animals often play a prominent role.

3. Language is intentionally obscure and allusions deliberately cryptic.

4. Both political cartoons and apocalyptic imag-ery refer specifically to a particular moment in time.

The book of Daniel is best understood as a prod-uct and reflection of its historical context. We should consequently acknowledge that the original audience was likely able to understand the book of Daniel more easily than we do. Hewitt uses a more recent historical example to illustrate this point:[6] During the Vietnam War, when American naval pilots were captured and pressured by their captors to name other pilots still operating, they responded with names such as Donald Duck, Mickey Mouse, and other Walt Disney figures. The captives' responses were then broadcast to the world, while the Vietnamese remained unaware that the replies were fictional characters. In effect, the pilots creatively used their enemies to relay a coded message that they were still alive and also in peril. In a similar way, we, as modern readers, can understand the overarching message of the book of Daniel—that the community is in danger but still alive and well—but we lose many of the finer points that require deep familiarity with the specific historical situation of the exilic community.

Although the book contains two distinct portions (Dan 1–6; 7–12), two different arguments can be made for the book's overall coherence. First, Daniel 7:1; 8:1; 9:1; 10:1; and 11:1 coincide with the narrative framework offered in the court-tales section of the book and also provide coherent transitions similar to those found throughout chapters 1–6. Second, the conclusion of the first section—"So Daniel prospered during the reign of Darius and the reign of Cyrus the Persian" (6:28)—echoes the last verse of the second portion of the book: "But you, Daniel, go on to the end; for you shall rest and stand in your lot at the end of the days" (12:13, my translation). This summary and blessing draw together the two major sections of the book, signaling to the reader that the book is to be read in its entirety and as a coherent whole.

Reading the Six Court Tales (Chapters 1–6)

Chapter 1: Daniel and His Friends in the King's Court

Among all the characters in this chapter, Jehoiakim, king of Judah (reigned 609–597 BC), is the only one who is faceless and voiceless. His mention in verse 1 frames the dramatic irony: God is behind both Jehoiakim's defeat and the victory of the Babylonian king Nebuchadnezzar over Judah. In a repetition that builds intensity within the story, verses 2 and 9 emphasize that it is God who is behind the exile, as well as the preservation of Daniel and his friends in the Babylonian court:

> "And the Lord *gave* Jehoiakim the king of
> Judah into his [Nebuchadnezzar's] hand"
> (v. 2a, my translation).

> "Now God had *given* Daniel kindness and compassion before the chief of the eunuchs" (v. 9, my translation; or "Now God *had caused the official* to show favor and compassion to Daniel," NIV).

With God's enabling, Daniel and his three friends passed the ten-day trial of refraining from royal food (vv. 10–16).[7] This emphasis is again picked up in the summary appraisal in verse 17: "To these four young men God *gave* knowledge and understanding of all kinds of literature and learning."

Daniel's exceptional characteristics also stand out among his three friends. The narrator's comment in verse 17 introduces Daniel's God-given ability to interpret dreams and visions, which he will use for various kings in chapters 2, 4, and 5. He serves as the mind (1:8) and the mouthpiece of this elite group in negotiating (1:12–13). The narrator provides a glimpse of Daniel's inner quality as a public figure—he is a man of determination. Using the wordplay of "set on/fixed/set,"[8] the text draws a comparison between the chief of the Babylonian officials "fixing/setting" a new Babylonian name for each of the young men (v. 7) and Daniel's inward act of determination in "setting on" his heart the conviction that he would not defile himself with the king's food or wine (v. 8). Verse 21 sums up Daniel's success: "And Daniel remained there until the first year of King Cyrus"—that is, 539 BC, meaning that he experienced the rule of three empires (Babylonian, Median, Persian) and four kings (Nebuchadnezzar, Belshazzar, Darius, and Cyrus). On the one hand, the summary appraisal in verse 21 serves as a prelude to Daniel's success in subsequent chapters; on the other hand, the major character in this first court tale is neither Daniel, nor king Nebuchadnezzar, but the Lord God—underscoring that it is God who brings about all these events.

JEWISH AND BABYLONIAN NAMES IN DANIEL[9]

Jewish Name	Babylonian Name
Daniel	Belteshazzar
Hananiah	Shadrach
Mishael	Meshach
Azariah	Abednego

Chapter 2: Daniel Interprets a Dream

Chapter 2 begins with a challenge to the Babylonian magicians, enchanters, sorcerers, and astrologists in the royal court over their inability to tell and interpret the dream of Nebuchadnezzar—the dream of an enormous statue made of gold, silver, bronze, and iron. By this time, Daniel's status is established: He is one who has direct access to the king's court (vv. 16, 24-25a), but at the same time his life and the lives of his companions are under threat (v. 13). In verses 17-18, Daniel urges his three friends to plead for God's mercy concerning the mystery of the dream. The doxology of praise to God in verses 20-23 stands in sharp contrast with Daniel's words to the king in his interpretation of the dream: "Your Majesty, you are the kings of kings. The God of heaven *has given* you dominion and power and might and glory; in your hands he has placed all mankind and the beasts of the field and the birds in the sky. Wherever they live, he *has made you* ruler over them all" (vv. 37-38a). Nebuchadnezzar's acknowledgement that God has enabled Daniel to interpret the dream further underscores the message of this chapter: that even kings who do not worship the God of Israel and Judah will proclaim, "Surely your God is the God of gods and the Lord of kings and a revealer of mysteries" (v. 47). Chapter 2 ends with Daniel's promotion to a high position in the royal court, along with his three friends, who become administrators in the province of Babylon (vv. 48-49).

IMPORTANT PLACES IN THE BABYLONIAN AND PERSIAN EMPIRES

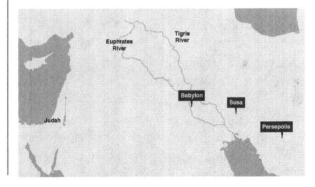

The way that the story progresses—from threat to resolution to the elevation of Daniel and his friends, and from the revelation of the dream to the king's acknowledgement of God's enabling power— is the narrator's way of posing the question, "Who is sovereign?" Then, of course, the narrative leads readers right to the answer. The One who gave Nebuchadnezzar dominion, power, might, and glory—the God of gods and Lord of kings—is the real sovereign.

Chapter 3: Delivery from the Furnace

Chapter 3 is a lively depiction of how Daniel's three friends introduced in chapter 1—Shadrach, Meshach, and Abednego—survived the fiery furnace experience through God's intervention. Daniel is totally absent from this chapter; instead, his three friends are mentioned by their individual names and also together as a group no less than thirteen times (vv. 12, 13, 14, 16, 19, 20, 22, 23, 26 [2 times], 28, 29, 30). On the surface, the three friends and King Nebuchadnezzar, who built a large image of gold to be worshiped, are center stage in this famous story. However, when the king's question in verse 15, "Then what god will be able to rescue you from my hand?" is echoed in verse 29, "For no other god can save in this way," it is revealed that the Hebrew God who miraculously delivered Shadrach, Meshach, and Abednego is the one truly at the center of this beautifully crafted narrative.

Chapter 3 is a multivoiced (or "multivocal" or "polyphonic") text, which means that many different perspectives are represented within the story, all of which present their own take on the events in the narrative.[10] If we pay attention to the number of voices present in the text, we find that chapter 3 is very "loud." Through sharp contrast and repetition, the interplay of these voices highlights the core message of the chapter and the point of view of the narrator.

There are five distinct voices within Daniel 3, some of which are collective.

1. The voice of King Nebuchadnezzar gives decrees (vv. 1, 13–15, 19) and astonished inquiries (vv. 24–26) and exclamations (vv. 28–29). Nebuchadnezzar's voice shifts from that of a dominant sovereign to that of a king humbled by the miraculous saving power of the Hebrew God, thus symbolizing a change of heart.

2. The voice of the herald (vv. 4–6) is loud and direct in carrying out the decrees of the king. The herald adheres to and advances the king's ideal—that people and nations of *all* languages should bow down and worship the image erected by the king.

3. Complementing the decreeing voice of the king and his herald is the sound of different musical instruments (horn, flute, zither, lyre, harp, pipes, and all kinds of music).[11]

4. The voice of the astrologers is one of accusation—the voice of conspiracy. Due to envy or jealousy, they seek to accuse the three faithful young men.

5. Lastly, there is the collective voice of Daniel's three friends. They stand as the voice of the faithful who speak boldly on God's behalf when confronting the king (vv. 16–18).

As stated previously, repetition is a literary device used throughout the Bible to emphasize certain points. There are seven sets of repetition in

Daniel 3 that highlight the splendor of the image that King Nebuchadnezzar set up as well as the severity of Shadrach, Meshach, and Abednego's punishment and deliverance: (1) the status of officials and staff who support the king's decree (vv. 2, 3, 27); (2) the phrase, "the image of gold that the king has set up" (vv. 2, 3, 5, 12, 14, 15, 18); (3) the listing of the musical instruments (vv. 5, 7, 10, 15); (4) the phrase "bow down and worship" (vv. 6, 7b, 10, 11, 14b); (5) the mention of *all* nations and people of *all* languages (vv. 4, 7); (6) the description of the burning furnace (vv. 6, 11, 15, 17, 21); and (7) the mention of the individual names of Daniel's three friends (vv. 12, 13, 14, 16, 19, 20, 22, 26, 28, 29, 30).

Toward the end of the chapter, the narrative takes an ironic twist. The two distinct and contrasting ideologies collapse into one—for there is no other God who can deliver like this but the God of Shadrach, Meshach, and Abednego (v. 29, compare also v. 15). This is a powerful answer to the question posed by King Nebuchadnezzar in verse 15, "Then who is that god who shall deliver you out of my hand?" (my translation). It is King Nebuchadnezzar himself who provides the answer to that question.

Chapter 4: Another Dream and Its Interpretation

Unique to chapter 4 is its structure, with the praise/ doxology of Nebuchadnezzar bracketing the story at the beginning (vv. 1-3) in the form of a decree and at the end in the form of a concluding doxology (vv. 34-35). The events that follow the opening praise are: (1) the dream report and the search for an interpreter (vv. 4-18); (2) Daniel's interpretation of the dream (vv. 19-27); (3) the fulfillment of the dream

(vv. 28–33); and (4) the restoration of Nebuchadnezzar and his concluding doxology (vv. 34–37). Through the unfolding of these events, this court tale aims to encourage and give confidence to the community of faith by demonstrating that, in spite of their helplessness before a seemingly all-powerful human ruler, the king is far from being the most powerful one. It is *God* who is in control, and he works on behalf of his people.

The dream report and the search for an interpreter (vv. 4–18): In his first-person, emphatic voice ("I, Nebuchadnezzar"), the king discloses the details of his dream (v. 5). Matching the style of the first-person visionary reports of chapters 7–12, Nebuchadnezzar informs the reader of the emotional impact that the dream has had on him: He is terrified and troubled (v. 5). Daniel is introduced and acknowledged in verse 9 as (a) the "chief of the magicians" (b) who has "the spirit of the holy gods" in him, while (c) "no mystery is too difficult for [him]." As Longman comments, this chapter may be interpreted as a tale of court contest (see also Exod 7:8–13) but in a subdued way. It silently shows that Daniel has succeeded while the other Babylonian diviners have failed.[12] The reason for Daniel's success is already known to the reader, because Daniel 1:17 reveals that his ability to interpret dreams is granted by God. Daniel 3 marks the first time that this is revealed to the Babylonian court.

The interpretation of the dream (vv. 19–27): The story then continues with a third-person narrator. The dynamic between Daniel and King Nebuchadnezzar is a remarkable one. Daniel hesitates to reveal the full meaning of the dream to the king, as he himself is that tree, or also the subject of the dream—God's coming judgment. At the conclusion of his interpretation, Daniel offers advice and counsel to the king in the hope that Nebuchadnezzar may escape divine judgment—a hope that is ultimately stifled by Nebuchadnezzar's disobedience (vv. 28–33). The call for repentance in verse 27 establishes the basis for God's impending judgment, as foretold in the dream.

The fulfillment of the dream (vv. 28–33): Verse 28 reports the fulfillment by first summarizing it in a simple, straightforward way—"All [these events] happened to King Nebuchadnezzar"—and then relating the details of the tragic events, which happen twelve months after Daniel's interpretation (vv. 29–33). While walking on the roof of his palace, Nebuchadnezzar marvels at its grandeur and says to himself, "Is not this the great Babylon I have built as the royal residence, by my mighty power and for the glory of my majesty?" (v. 30). Nebuchadnezzar's refusal to repent and humble himself brings about the immediate fulfillment of the tragic prediction.

Restoration and concluding doxology (vv. 34–37): The narrative ends with the tale of the king's restoration as well as a concluding doxology from the mouth of King Nebuchadnezzar himself. In a turn of events, the mighty power, glory, and majesty in the self-reflection of the king (as recorded in v. 30) are now offered to God, addressing him whose dominion is eternal and whose kingdom endures forever (v. 34). He is the supreme sovereign, and "no one can hold back his hand" (v. 35b).

The moral of the story is at the last word: "Those who walk in pride he is able to humble" (v. 37b). This is brought to the foreground as the narrator intentionally casts a sharp contrast between the mighty Babylonian king Nebuchadnezzar[13] and the everlasting dominion and majestic kingdom of the Hebrew God. It provides another powerful answer to the question, "Who is sovereign?"

Chapter 5: The Writing on the Wall

Chapter 5 begins abruptly, with the introduction of Belshazzar[14] to the Babylonian court. In chapter 3, King Nebuchadnezzar *made* a great image of gold. Here in chapter 5, Belshazzar *makes*[15] a great feast for his nobles and commands that they drink from the same holy vessels that his predecessor, Nebuchadnezzar, brought from the temple in Jerusalem (vv. 1–4). During the feast, the fingers of a human hand appear and write on the plaster of the wall (v. 5). Out of desperation and panic, the king orders his entire council to read and interpret the writing. When all efforts fail, the king is exceedingly terrified (v. 9), but Daniel is introduced by the queen mother (vv. 10–13). The chapter continues with Daniel's speech of accusation, followed by the interpretation of the writing, which carries a message of doom. Finally, the chapter ends abruptly with the revelation of Belshazzar's fate: "That very night Belshazzar, king of the Babylonians, was slain, and Darius the Mede took over the kingdom" (5:30–31).

If chapter 2 is about a contest between an earthly sovereign and the Hebrew God, chapter 5 may be perceived as a competition between weak King Belshazzar and the competent Daniel, who has a measure of control over the king because of his ability to interpret. This competition is especially evident when one focuses on the narrator's portrayal of the king's reaction after witnessing the writing on the wall in verse 6. In a vivid manner, the text states that his color was changed and his thoughts troubled him, "and he was so frightened that his legs became weak and his knees were knocking" (v. 6).[16] This sharply contrasts with the competent and courageous spirit of Daniel, which is demonstrated in his long speech of accusation to the king.

THE WRITING ON THE WALL

The phrase described as being written on the wall of the banquet hall in 5:25 was "Mene, Mene, Tekel, Parsin." The words in this enigmatic Aramaic phrase are probably related to units of measure, making the meaning, "a mina, a mina, a shekel, and two halves." Daniel's interpretation played on the meaning of the words, predicting the fall of Babylon close at hand: "*Mene*: God has numbered" (v. 26); "*Tekel*: You have been weighed" (v. 27); "*Peres*: Your kingdom is divided" (v. 28).[17]

It is through this contrast that the power of Daniel's God, the one who brings about the immediate fulfillment of doom, looms large. The events of this chapter give another powerful answer to the question, "Who is truly sovereign?" The answer: the God of Daniel.

Chapter 6: The Lions' Den

The narrator intentionally puts Daniel at center stage in chapter 6, and it is God's miraculous rescue of Daniel that demonstrates the sovereignty of God. Daniel's bold voice of condemnation in chapter 5 now becomes a silent voice of resistance. Reading Daniel 1-6 as resistance literature and as a survival manual, we can see that the coping strategy that Daniel adopts here is a fearless yet silent resistance to the conspiracy against him (vv. 10-13). His public role as an aspiring sage and his status as the third most powerful man in the kingdom have been firmly established. Moreover, he has distinguished himself among the other leaders (administrators and satraps) and shown that he is a man with "an extraordinary spirit" (v. 3, NASB). By contrast, the Median king Darius is depicted as a weak king manipulated by his own officials (vv. 6-9).

Daniel gains Darius' favor; Darius actually expresses displeasure with himself and conveys his wish for Daniel's God to rescue him from the lions' den (vv. 14, 16, 18). Daniel is aware of the king's wishes (vv. 16, 20) and confident that God will shut the mouths of the lions, so he remains calm in the face of danger (vv. 10, 21-22).

The power, dominion, and sovereignty of God in this court tale are further established through King Darius' universal decree: "*All* the nations and peoples of *every* language in *all* the earth" (v. 25)[18] are to fear and revere the God of Daniel.[19] This is a complete reversal of the universal decree ordered by Nebuchadnezzar in chapter 3—for *all* peoples from *all* nations and of *all* languages to bow down and worship the image of gold that he had erected (see vv. 2-7).

Conclusion

The first portion of the book of Daniel—the six court tales—ends with an affirming doxology praising God's eternal kingdom and everlasting dominion (6:26–27). This affirmation serves as the prevailing message and conclusion of the first half of the book. The God of Daniel; the God of Shadrach, Meshach, and Abednego; the God of the captive Jewish community and each of the foreign kings is the sovereign God. This is the central theme—he is the God of gods and Lord of lords.

SUGGESTED READING

☐   Read the whole of Daniel 1–6, paying particular attention to words and phrases that emphasize God's sovereignty.

Reflection

As you engage in reading the six court tales, identify the ways that the theme of God's sovereignty is brought to the forefront in each.

_____

_____

_____

_____

What does it mean for you to put your trust in and submit yourself to a sovereign God?

FROM THE
EARTHLY TO THE
HEAVENLY REALM

Chapter 7 marks the major transition to the second
portion of the book of Daniel (chs. 7–12). The first six
chapters are court tales narrated in the third person;
the last six are reports of apocalyptic visions narrated
in the first person. In the first half, we learn of the
faith and perseverance of Daniel and his three friends
before foreign kings, and we witness God's miraculous interventions. God is in control of the fate of his
people. In the second half of the book, we move from
the present circumstances of God's people in captivity
to their ultimate liberation. This textual development
creates a shift in focus from human evils performed
by the foreign kings and their court officials to the
perverse spiritual forces that stand behind them. This
transition moves from deliverance out of a burning
furnace and a den of lions in chapters 1–6 to eternal
resurrection and inheritance for the people of God in
the concluding chapter of the book (12:13).[1]

In chapters 1–6, the narrator tells us that everything happened exactly how the sovereign God

determined. Chapters 7–12, however, are written in the first-person voice of Daniel. With his emphatic references to himself (that is, "I, Daniel," in 7:15, 28; 8:27; 10:2, 7; 12:5), Daniel invites the audience—both the original, sixth-century BC community in captivity as well as contemporary readers—to immerse themselves in his visionary experience.[2] As discussed in chapter 2, the nonchronological arrangement of the chapters in the book underscores the transition between the two distinct literary portions (court tales and apocalyptic writings). The transition is smooth and seamless, with the sovereign God's earthly activities highlighted in chapters 1–6 and his activities in the heavenly realm described in chapters 7–12.

Approaching the Apocalyptic Section of Daniel (Chapters 7–12)

The second portion of the book shows characteristic features of apocalyptic literature as Daniel reports his visions concerning the future. These visions are full of mysterious images, exotic descriptions of celestial figures, puzzling numbers, and indeterminate timetables. While readers' active participation in the meaning-making process of the first six chapters is crucial, reading chapters 7–12 requires a deeper level of emotional engagement with the first-person visions.

In other words, readers are encouraged to immerse themselves in Daniel's visionary experience as he describes it. The way in which the passage requires readers' involvement is, perhaps, the key to understanding the significance of each of the four visions (7:1–28; 8:1–27; 9:23–27; 10:1–12:13).

The implications of this approach are threefold. First, in spite of the mystifying nature of the visions—which are far from possible to interpret with any precision—Daniel never pauses to uncover their meanings with the angels' help. He watches attentively and eagerly awaits the revelation of their meanings (7:6, 9, 11, 13, 19, 20; 8:3, 4, 5, 13, 15, 19, 20; 10:5, 7; 12:5, 8). Second, he admits that in spite of his desire to know more, the visions and their interpretations by heavenly messengers are beyond his understanding (7:15, 28; 8:27). Third, the emotional impact upon him is so profound (7:15, 28; 8:27; 10:7–11) that he is appalled by the visions, lies ill for several days, and remains in a state of great distress for some time. In other words, the experiential and emotional dimension of Daniel's visions provide an opportunity for the audience to connect with both the prophet and the awe-inspiring visions of the divine that he shares.

Daniel's visions can be understood up to a point, but as readers today, we can't completely comprehend all of the details. Many of the finer points likely were lost on the ancient audience as well, given the cryptic nature of the visions and their messages. Grasping the full extent of the interpretation of the visions and the apocalyptic timetables[3] with any precision should not be regarded as an interpretive priority, as it is beyond our reach (perhaps by design). As C. M. Kempton has commented, "Any attempt to understand the apocalypses better must begin with humility and awe."[4] The attitude of human inadequacy to comprehend the full meaning of the symbols, dreams, and exotic visions is the *right* attitude (compare 7:13–14, 17–18, 19–20, 28; 8:15, 26, 27; 12:5–13, esp. vv. 8–9). Though the visions clearly affirm that the sovereign God is in control, they leave us in suspense at times and uncertain about specifics.

Before we dive more deeply into the apocalyptic material in the book of Daniel, let's describe apocalyptic literature in more detail. Scholars sometimes identify the following key characteristics of apocalyptic literature.[5] While not all works belonging to this genre have all of these characteristics, all of them are present in Daniel 7–12:

- the unveiling of a divine plan through visions or dreams
- detailed description(s) of past and present events, often in coded language
- a detailed description of "the end times," including a chronology of surreal events
- a sharp contrast between the forces of light/good and the forces of darkness/evil
- pessimism regarding the present; optimism regarding future victory and divine transformation of the cosmos (compare Rev 21:1)
- mythic, chaotic, war imagery, often alluding to other ancient Near Eastern traditions; God is truly triumphant, and his victory is eternal
- surreal and metarealistic imagery[6]

We will find all of these characteristics as we walk through Daniel's four exotic visions.

Glimpses into the Mystery of the Sovereign God

Connecting the book of Daniel to our own lives is easier if we imagine three "worlds" as we examine the text and then look at how each world affects interpretation.[7] These three worlds are:

1. the world behind the text;

2. the world of/within the text; and

3. the world in front of the text.

In the world *behind* the text of the book of Daniel, we focus on issues related to the historical, cultural, and ideological backgrounds of the sixth century BC— when the Jewish people were in captivity. The world *of/within* the text is the literary dimension of the text. The world *in front of* the text is the most reader-oriented of these three worlds of biblical interpretation. Reader-oriented approaches focus on the importance of the readers' role in interpretation, empowering and encouraging all readers to bring our individual selves to the meaning-making process. As it is often said, meaning-making happens at the intersection of text and reader.

We will keep this "three-world" approach in mind as we walk through the four visions, navigating between the three worlds. It's also helpful to take an experiential approach to the text and embrace the experience of reading, especially in reading the apocalyptic chapters (chs. 7–12). We'll immerse ourselves in Daniel's descriptions of God as the "Ancient of Days," "the Most High," and the "luminous man" of chapters 7 and 10, and be drawn to the power and sovereignty of God as illustrated in Daniel's visions.

Chapter 7: The Four Beasts and the "Son of Man"

The first vision that Daniel receives comes during the first year of Belshazzar's reign (v. 1; probably around 553 BC). This precise historical setting links the earthly realm to the heavenly realm in Daniel's exotic visions. In this vision, Daniel witnesses four horrifying and powerful beasts coming up out of the sea: a lion, a bear, a leopard, and an enigmatic, ten-horned beast. This is a frightening scene, as each of the four beasts is extraordinary—a lion with the wings of an eagle that can stand on two feet like a man and is given a man's heart (NIV "mind of a human"; v. 4); a bear with three ribs between its teeth (v. 5); and a four-headed leopard with four wings on its back (v. 6). Significantly distinct from the other beasts, the fourth is the most terrifying and devastating. It has iron teeth and ten horns, crushes and devours its victims, and tramples underfoot whatever is left. There is another, little horn that comes up after three of the first ten horns are uprooted. This small horn has the eyes of a man and a mouth that speaks boastfully (vv. 7–8).

While Daniel looks in terror at the emergence of the little horn, a vision about the Ancient of Days is revealed to him. The symbolism used to describe the Ancient of Days is that of purity ("His clothing was as white as snow; the hair of his head was white like wool" [7:9a]); majesty ("His throne was flaming with fire, and its wheels were all ablaze" [7:9b]; "A river of fire was flowing, coming out from before him"

[7:10a]); and royalty ("Thousands upon thousands attended him; ten thousand times ten thousand stood before him" [7:10b]). Verse 10c vividly describes this pure, majestic, and royal figure, the Ancient of Days, as a judge in a courtroom: "The court was seated, and the books were opened" (v. 10c). While Daniel watches, the beast with the little horn is slain and the other three beasts are stripped of their authority (v. 11). This outcome as specified in verses 11-12 is a direct result of the judgment of the heavenly court: "The court was seated, and the books were opened" (v. 10c); "The other beasts had been stripped of their authority, but were *allowed* to live for a period of time" (v. 12).

It is meaningful that the vision in verses 13-14 follows immediately after the verdict. Daniel looks, and there is one "like a son of man"[8] arriving "with the clouds of heaven" (v. 13). He approaches the Ancient of Days and is given authority, glory, and sovereign power—all peoples, nations, and men of every language worship him (a sharp contrast to the decree of King Nebuchadnezzar in chapter 3). This second heavenly figure fits well with the depiction of a sovereign king who is given all power and authority to rule and is the subject of worship for all peoples. He demolishes all of the destructive powers and authorities represented by the four beasts—he is a true sovereign with everlasting dominion, whose kingdom will never be destroyed (v. 14).

The interpretation of this twofold vision follows after Daniel asks for the meaning (v. 16). One of the heavenly beings whom Daniel witnesses offers him an explanation of three different elements of the vision:

- **The four beasts** (7:17) represent four chronological risings of empires, in accordance with their respective power and might.

- **The fourth beast** (7:23) represents the most devastating power among those four (vv. 24–25).

- **The ten horns** (7:24) are the ten kings who rise in the course of the fourth kingdom, and eventually, one super-king rises up and subdues the others. Verse 25 spells out the extent and nature of his destructive acts: "He will speak against the Most High and oppress his holy people and try to change the set times and the laws. The holy people will be delivered into his hands *for a time, times and half a time*" (v. 25).[9]

Based on the heavenly being's explanation, we have a good idea of the interpretation of this twofold dream vision. Focusing on the world behind the text, we see that Daniel and the original audience are still in captivity in the Babylonian Empire (v. 1). All of the predicted risings of kings and empires are yet to be fulfilled; the full impact of the happenings is yet to be realized on the stage of history. Identifying the four beasts' historical identities has been the subject of heated debate in the history of interpretation of the book of Daniel. For example, a key discussion focuses on whether the fourth beast represents the kingdom of Greece (after Persia) or Rome (after Greece). Commentators who hold to the Greek interpretation commonly identify the climactic little horn as Antiochus IV Epiphanes, who actively oppressed the Jewish people in the middle of the second century BC— defiling the temple, prohibiting Jewish practice, and banning circumcision. This inspired a major revolt (the Maccabean Revolt) that resulted in a century of semiautonomous rule in Judea under the Hasmonean dynasty.[10]

Looking at the world within the text, the essence of verses 16–27 is: (1) There is an earthly war as well as a cosmic war between the beasts and the saints of the Most High,[11] with the Most High God and the Ancient of Days fighting for them (vv. 21, 22). (2) The focus is on the devastating acts of the fourth beast and the little horn (vv. 17, 19, 20–21, 23–25) and the outcomes of its destructive actions (vv. 21, 25–26). (3) The final victory of the saints of the Most High is foretold in verse 18, before Daniel sees the little horn waging war against the saints and defeating them (v. 21). Moreover, the pronouncement of judgment by the Ancient of Days on behalf of the saints of the Most High comes before the full manifestation of the oppressive acts performed by the king (the little horn) arising from the fourth kingdom (v. 22). This sequence of events thus creates an element of suspense for both the original audience and emotionally engaged modern readers, as it promises protection against the coming of doom. (4) The final verdict from the court is spelled out in verses 26–27: "His power will be taken away and completely destroyed forever. Then the sovereignty, power and greatness of all the kingdoms under heaven will be handed over to the holy people of the Most High. His kingdom will be an everlasting kingdom, and all rulers will worship and obey him." What a glorious final victory!

As we readers—amidst wars, conflicts, injustice, human suffering, and aggressions of superpowers against the weak and needy—seek to turn our reading into a dialogue with the world of Daniel, just like Daniel we watch and experience the impact of earthly powers on humanity and are troubled and disturbed by what we witness (v. 15). Sometimes we keep these matters to ourselves (v. 28), as we need time to process our feelings. Perhaps that is why the promises and the pronouncement of judgment are intermingled with the interpretation in verses 16–27. In the midst of the continuous unfolding of tragic events, time and again we are reminded that God will bring about the final victory on behalf of his people. The sovereign God is still in control and determines a set time for human suffering: "A time, times, and half a time" (v. 25).

> In the midst of the continuous unfolding of tragic events, time and again we are reminded that God will bring about the final victory on behalf of his people.

As Goldingay has observed, this chapter ends in perplexity (v. 28). It serves to encourage us, even though we find ourselves confused about the key details of the vision. If we think we have grasped and clearly understood it, that may well be a sign that we're actually misunderstanding it.[12]

Chapter 8: A Ram and a Goat

Daniel's vision of a ram and a goat occurs during the third year of King Belshazzar's reign (Dan 8:1; probably around 551 BC); his presence in Susa may be understood as transportation in spirit (compare Ezek 8). Focusing on the world within the text, readers can see that this symbolic vision is full of astrological symbolism, which was common in the ancient world: The ram and the goat represent constellations.

The general structure of the vision is as follows: (1) the circumstances and setting of the vision (vv. 1-2); (2) Daniel's first-person report, which opens with "behold" (my translation; vv. 3-12); (3) the angelic discourse (vv. 13-14); (4) the epiphany of the interpreter (vv. 15-17); (5) the interpretation (vv. 19-25); and (6) the concluding description of Daniel's reaction (v. 27).

This vision focuses first on the might and ferocity of the ram—it does whatever it pleases and becomes very great—and then the rage between the ram and the goat occupies center stage. The powerful ram is attacked furiously, and when its two horns are shattered, it becomes powerless (v. 7). The goat then becomes very great, but at the height of its power, its large horn is broken. In its place, four prominent horns grow up, and out of them another horn comes up, growing to be very powerful. A series of destructive events showing the extent of its power (vv. 10-12) depicts a master of devastation acting against the sanctuary of God and targeting the people of God. The horn prospers in everything it does, without any restraints (v. 12). Then comes the discourse between two angelic beings (holy ones) over the question, "How long will it take for the vision to be fulfilled?" (v. 13). Their conversation climaxes at the answer to this question: "It will take 2,300 *evenings and mornings*; then the sanctuary will be reconsecrated" (v. 14).

On the one hand, the time period of 2,300 evenings and mornings is both precise and determinate in its method of calculation—"evening and morning" (perhaps the unit of a day).[13] On the other hand, we lack any concrete reference point as to when to begin counting.[14] The significance of these 2,300 evenings and mornings is in the phrase's precision and certainty, but also in that God alone knows the timing of his deliverance. When this time period was revealed to Daniel and the first audience, they did not know when exactly deliverance would come, but they did know that it was guaranteed.

Daniel's attempt to understand the vision is fulfilled by a named angelic being, Gabriel (v. 17). Before the interpretation identifying the ram and the goat, Daniel is terrified and falls prostrate. He then falls into a deep sleep with his face to the ground, then is raised by Gabriel onto his feet. Gabriel indicates to him twice that the vision "concerns the time of the end" (vv. 17b, 19) and "concerns the distant future" (v. 26). Because of Gabriel's specific interpretation in verses 20-21, even the original audience, under the reign of Belshazzar, would have grasped the precise identification of the ram and the goat, as well as the horns: Daniel 8:20-21 clarifies that the two-horned ram represents the kings of Media and Persia, the goat is the king of Greece, and the large horn between its eyes is the first king—Alexander the Great. The four horns that replace the large horn are the less-powerful generals who succeeded Alexander upon his death in 323 BC and divided the empire into four.[15]

The "completely wicked," "fierce-looking king, a master of intrigue" (vv. 23-25) has been identified by many as Antiochus IV, who may also be the little horn of Daniel 7.[16] His evil acts and merciless destruction fit with the vision's portrayal of him in Daniel 7:8, 11, though no specific interpretation is given in Daniel 8.

However, this passage's assurances—that there is a determined period of time for the fulfillment (8:14); that the fulfillment of the vision concerns "the time of the end" (v. 17b) and "the distant future" (v. 26); and that the wicked master of intrigue will be destroyed, though *not by human power* (v. 25b)—all point to certainty that the vision will be fulfilled at the appointed time.

As we think about our own world in light of Daniel's experience, we notice that he looks, hears, and tries to understand the full impact of the vision (vv. 3, 5, 13, 15, 16) but is terrified and cannot help but fall down (v. 17b). In his summary statement (v. 27), he indicates that he is totally worn out after his visionary experience and has lain ill for several days. Furthermore, Daniel admits that the vision dismays him, for it is beyond his understanding.

As we seek to immerse ourselves in Daniel's visionary experience, we should be careful not to make the identities of the astrological figures (like the ram and the goat) central to our meaning-making. Rather, chapter 8 provides us with the following assurances: (1) that the sanctuary will be reconsecrated after 2,300 evenings and mornings (v. 14); (2) that the details of the vision are true (v. 26); and (3) that the power of the sovereign God will bring about the destruction of the evil powers (v. 25b). Thanks to these assurances, Daniel is able to set aside the emotional impact the vision has upon him, get up, and go about his job in service of King Belshazzar (v. 27a).

Chapter 9: Daniel's Prayer of Confession and Jeremiah's Prophecy

Chapter 8 concludes the symbolic representations of the future contained within the book of Daniel. As in the previous chapters, chapter 9 begins with a concrete historical reference: the first year of Darius the Mede's reign (v. 1; 539 BC; compare Dan 5:30-31). In verse 2, Daniel seeks to understand his own circumstances and turns to the prophecy of Jeremiah, declaring that the exile in Babylon will last for seventy years (Jer 25:8-14). Daniel performs the usual ritual of repentance—"in prayer and petition, in fasting, and in sackcloth and ashes" (v. 3).

The chapter then continues with one of the most outstanding penitential prayers in the Old Testament (vv. 3-19; compare also Neh 9:5-37; Ezra 9:6-15). At first, we might think that the placement of this prayer within the apocalyptic portion of the book is odd. However, the prayer functions as a shift between the earthly dreams and their interpretations by Daniel in chapters 1-6, which are paired with his own visions in 7-8, and the visions that follow in 10-12; between the worldly conflicts and the cosmic wars in which spiritual forces are the contestants. The prayer underscores that the sovereignty of God is behind all these.

Focusing on the world within the text, the reader can see that Daniel's prayer of confession contains a rich portrayal of the God of Israel. Through a lengthy telling of the mighty hand of God (v. 15) working in the history of Israel—deliverance from slavery in Egypt, judgments, and exiles—Daniel describes God as he has been experienced by the people of Israel. In essence, the confessional prayer strategically connects the sovereignty of God as witnessed by Daniel with his historical context of exile and with its continuous manifestation as anticipated in the last vision (chs. 10–12).

God is addressed as the "great and awesome God" and "the Lord of the covenant" (v. 4, my translation). The prayer highlights the history of Israel and Judah's rebellion and their refusal to repent (vv. 4–14). Since God is righteous and just—as portrayed in the court scene of chapter 7 where the Ancient of Days presides and upholds the covenant he made with the people of Judah—the exile to Babylon is the final and fair punishment he exacts on his people for their stubbornness. Daniel repeatedly uses the mighty hand of God in describing the nation's exodus experience and portrays God as a redeemer who enabled Israel to walk through the bottom of the Red Sea on dry ground (Exod 14:16, 22, 29) and who chose to become their covenant God (Exod 19–20).

The most striking feature in this prayer is the four imperatives in verse 19—"Lord, *listen!* Lord, *forgive!* Lord, *hear* and *act!*" This plea has two main goals: (1) God's great mercy; and (2) that the desolate sanctuary, city, and the people of Judah would all bear God's name. The urgency and sorrowful petition for God's action ("look with favor … give ear … and hear; open your eyes and see," vv. 17–18) correspond well with the urgency of the revelation of the seventy "sevens" by Gabriel in verses 20–27.

Also notice: This is the first time that Daniel's own initiative results in a revelation—the vision of the seventy "sevens." The word "while" is used twice in verses 20–21, signifying an immediate, heavenly response to Daniel's prayer of confession ("a word went out," v. 23). The vision about the seventy "sevens" is meant to be interpreted using the insight and understanding provided by the archangel Gabriel. Gabriel reinterprets the seventy years in Jeremiah's prophecy (Jer 25:8–14) as seventy "sevens." However, like the 2,300 days and nights in Daniel 7, we have no way of knowing what, exactly, this timeframe corresponds to.

In the world of the text, and without making any attempt to relate this heavenly secret to any future historical events, the reader can see that Gabriel's reinterpretation outlines six events that will come to pass:[17] (1) the end of transgression; (2) the end of sin;[18] (3) the atonement for wickedness; (4) the ushering in of everlasting righteousness; (5) the sealing of visions and prophecy; and (6) the anointing of the most holy place (v. 24). As Longman has noticed, the outlining of these events certainly sounds like an answer to Daniel's plea.[19] However, Daniel and his contemporaries only know of the imperfect, exilic world in which they are situated. The extermination of evil and the establishment of everlasting righteousness are ideals, only present in the distant future.

Gabriel further divides the coming days into two segments: (1) the restoration and rebuilding of Jerusalem and the coming of the Anointed One (the ruler) during the first seven "sevens," followed by another sixty-two "sevens" (v. 26) and (2) the last "seven" (or "seventieth seven") as a period of devastation, marked by the killing of the Anointed One, continuous wars, and destructive actions performed by a ruler, including the destruction of the city and sanctuary of Jerusalem. Toward the end of this last "seven," an unnamed ruler will bring desolation to the temple and worship (v. 27).

It is not surprising that the meaning of the seventy "sevens" has been much debated. Pinning down the historical reference of the phrase is difficult. Joyce Baldwin has pointed out that at the time of Daniel's vision and prayer, the end of the exile had not been realized yet, but chapter 9 reassures its readers that the sovereign God will be present in every crisis of his people; "the numbers are merely the 'clothing' of the writer's thoughts and are of no significance now."[20] The significance of Daniel's vision can be understood to a certain extent but not in full detail. What is certain is that the end of the period of suffering has already been decreed; it is only a matter of time until the vision comes to pass ("seventy 'sevens' are *decreed* for your people," 9:24; "until the end that is *decreed* is poured out on him," 9:27).

The lengthy historical recitation in Daniel's prayer sheds light on the significance of this vision. The redeemer God who has miraculously led the people of Israel through the Red Sea on dry ground with his mighty hand and outstretched arm (v. 15), the covenant God who has patiently guided his chosen people with his faithfulness (vv. 4–14), is the same God who, by his sovereignty, decrees the events and timing of all things.

Chapters 10–12: A Heavenly Messenger and a Great War

The last vision is Daniel's most terrifying, according to the narrator. Considering the world of the text, the reader can see that this passage has seven distinct characteristics:

1. The message given in the vision is true (10:1b);

2. It is about a great war, more or less of a cosmic nature (10:1b; ch. 11);

3. It is meant to be understood (10:1c, 12; 12:4, 5, 8);

4. It concerns the actual end times and may include specific numbers of days (10:14; 11:27b, 29, 35, 36b, 40; 12:4, 7b, 12, 13);

5. It concerns the future of God's people (10:4, 14; 12:1);

6. It reveals events at the end of the present era, beyond human history (12:4-13); and

7. Most importantly, it reveals that *it is certain* that a power will restrain evil forces and triumph.

Note the cluster of textual references in support of the last observation: "because his empire will be uprooted and given to others" (11:4); "In those days, she will be *betrayed*" (11:6); "the king of the South ... yet he will *not remain triumphant*" (11:12); "those who are violent among your own people will rebel ... but *without success*" (11:14); "but will *stumble and fall*, to be seen no more" (11:19); "he will plot the overthrow of fortresses—but *only for a time*" (11:24b); "the two kings ... will sit at the same table and lie to each other, but to *no avail*, because an *end* will still come *at the appointed time* (11:27); "but the people who know their God will *firmly resist* him" (11:32); "some of the wise will stumble, so that they may be refined, purified and made spotless until the time of the end, for it will still come *at the appointed time*" (11:35); "he will be successful until the *time of wrath* is completed, for what has been determined *must take place*" (11:36); "he will pitch his royal tents ... Yet he *will come to his end*, and no one will help him" (11:45).

Unpacking the events and how they correspond to the actions of the kings of the South and the North, with the same degree of detail, poses a challenge to all interpreters.[21] What, then, is the message of this last vision?

Looking at the three worlds of the text is a good starting point. In the world behind the text, this vision was given to Daniel in the third year of Cyrus, king of Persia (536 BC). With reference to 6:28, "Daniel prospered during the reign of Darius and the reign of Cyrus the Persian," and 11:1, "and in the first year of Darius the Mede, I took my stand to support and protect him." If Daniel's vision happened in the sixth century BC, then everything beginning with Daniel 11:1 can be regarded as a foretelling prophecy. Given the description of the mighty king in 11:3-4, the future regarding the kingdom of Greece and the emerging mighty sovereign can be linked to that empire's founder, Alexander the Great. The great war is waged between the South and the North (11:5-20). The contemptible person described in 11:21-45 is commonly thought to be the second-century BC Antiochus IV Epiphanes. From 11:5 onward, this last vision moves from the earthly (historical) events to be fulfilled in the near future (for instance, 11:3-4) to the final completion in the distant future through a great war—brought about by the power and determination of the sovereign God whose intervention is both heavenly and cosmic.

Interpreting the world of/within the text, 10:1 provides a framework for our construction of the sequence of events laid out in 10:2 to 12:13—the message is true, and it concerns a great war (10:1b); the vision is meant for the understanding of the heavenly message. After the introductory verses (10:1-2), the bulk of 10:1 to 11:1 is about Daniel's reaction to the vision of the great war. It is the most intense and elaborate of his first-person reports, and afterward, Daniel is in mourning for three weeks (10:2). The episode of this vision begins with a luminous man (10:4-6)— quite extraordinary, unlike any other description of the Holy One or God in the previous visions (compare 7:9-10). Every part of his appearance leaves us with the image of a radiant, royal man dressed in linen and precious goods, speaking with the voice of a multitude (compare 7:9-10). Both Ezekiel 1:26-28 and Revelation 1:12-16 portray the glory of God in a similar fashion, but Daniel's portrayal is perhaps the most awe-inspiring.

Daniel's reaction is one of terror and fear, to the extent that he is drained of all strength (10:7-9). Daniel begins his recollection of this vision by sharing with his audience the extreme psychological and physiological impact of this multilayered vision on him (10:2-11, 15-17). Then, he is empowered and strengthened (10:12-19). At the moment Daniel is overwhelmed with terror, the glorious man dressed in linen begins conversation with him (10:11-15). Next comes one who looks like a man (10:16, 18), and he also begins to talk with Daniel, strengthening him (10:16-19) and revealing to him events that will happen on the world stage, as well as the rise and fall of the kings of the North and South in the great war (10:20-11:45).

In chapter 12, the archangel Michael is mentioned as the great prince who protects God's people (12:1). There is an additional scene portraying two others standing on both sides of the river (12:5). One initiates a conversation with the other, standing above the water and dressed in linen (12:6-7). Daniel joins the conversation as he overhears the statement, "It will be for a time, times and half a time. When the power of the holy people has been finally broken, all these things will be completed" (12:7). Then another dialogue (12:8-9) continues out of the first, this time between one being standing on the shore and one standing above the water (12:5-7).

From the perspective of the world of/within the text, the multitude of celestial figures and multiplicity of voices speaking in both dialogue and monologue (10:2-11) exemplify the highly sophisticated structure of this vision report. Daniel 10:1 offers an interpretive link: "The understanding of the message came to him in a vision." In this vision, there is an attempt to present its meaning—the true message concerning the great war (10:1b)—in conversation with the various figures who speak with Daniel in the course of his vision (for example, 10:2-21; 12:5-9). The meaning of the vision is multilayered and quite complex; as in Daniel 3, it takes a multivocal approach to accommodate the many perspectives on its explanation and reception.[22]

Looking at the world in front of the text, readers can see that chapters 10-12 contain the vision of a heavenly conflict. On the one hand, the cosmic conflicts and battles with the king of Persia and then with the king of Greece represent the spiritual evils that support the human empires oppressing God's people. God and his powerful angels—especially Michael, a powerful spiritual being (11:1)—will fight for God's people and will bring about an eternal victory. Yet this will only be realized in the distant future, at the specific time(s) of deliverance. The overarching message is that judgment is *certain* for those who resist God and oppress his people. The equally certain truth is that God's people, downtrodden in the present, will experience final deliverance and new life in the fullest sense (12:1–3). The sequence of events in chapter 11 presents a sharp contrast between the kingdom and kingship of the earthly sovereigns and those of the Sovereign of sovereigns (11:36–45).

> God's people, downtrodden in the present, will experience final deliverance and new life in the fullest sense (12:1–3).

Today's readers put our world in conversation with the world of the text, particularly from Daniel's perspective, when we are drawn into the world of his inner life. In this last vision, he sees, hears, engages in conversation, is frightened, loses his strength, and is also touched, strengthened, and empowered by angels. He admits that the sequence of end-time events is beyond his understanding, but still he seeks to understand and initiate the inquiry of "how long" (12:6; compare Isa 6:11; 21:11; Pss 74:10; 82:2), only to be instructed to "roll up and seal the words of the scroll until the time of the end" (12:4, 9). Daniel is given a reward and inheritance, along with those who persevere (12:12), but is reminded to go on with the ordinary responsibilities of life (12:13). As we relate to Daniel in his visionary, fearful experience, we cannot help but reflect deeply and ask ourselves: Is it enough for us to go on with our ordinary life and persevere till the end, not knowing "how long"? After an emotionally explosive and exotic visionary experience, 12:13 presents a

> Is it enough for us to go on with our ordinary life and persevere till the end, not knowing "how long"?

calm, serene, but assuring hope: "As for you, [Brother John/Sister Mary], go your way till the end. You will rest, and then at the end of the days you will rise to receive your allotted inheritance" (my translation).

Approaching the four visions with the three worlds of the text in mind helps us create a bridge between the sixth-century exilic community, with its sufferings and expectation of a glorious future, and our own lives as we turn to the same text for guidance. As we read the four vision reports (chs. 7–12) after the six court tales (chs. 1–6), we can see the text transitioning from one section to the next in several areas: (1) from earthly to heavenly realms; (2) from suffering under hostile foreign rules to defeats and victories of a cosmic nature that involve heavenly intervention; (3) from the sovereignty of God exhibited through earthly events intermingled with kings and empires to the focus on the supreme sovereign of the universe; and (4) most importantly, from the affirmation of God's control over all earthly and heavenly decrees to the certainty of the truth of the future events. Using a variety of literary devices, the twelve chapters of the book of Daniel paint a complex portrait of God as the supreme sovereign. He is still in control over human evil and over conflicts on the cosmic level, even though things might look bleak from our perspective.

Understanding the Apocalyptic Timetables

Daniel is the only apocalyptic book that provides such specific chronologies of end-time events—particularly in chapters 8 and 11.[23] The key to understanding these timetables is to consider their function within their immediate and broader textual contexts. For Daniel's original audience, the timetables functioned not so much to provide theoretical information, but rather to console and encourage them.[24] In 12:11–12, the timetables are intended to provide the strength to persevere till the end. In the examples below, notice: As the inquirer's urgency increases (often in the form of a question), the answer also becomes more precise (for example, through the spelling out of the precise number of days).

EXAMPLE	LEAST
7:25: "for a time, times and half a time"	URGENT
CONTEXT	
"I approached one of those standing there and asked him the meaning of all this" (v. 16); "Then I wanted to know the meaning of the fourth beast" (v. 19); "I also wanted to know about the ten horns" (v. 20); "He gave me this explanation" (v. 23a)	

EXAMPLE

8:14: "It will take 2,300 evenings and mornings; then the sanctuary will be reconsecrated"

CONTEXT

"How long will it take for the vision to be fulfilled—the vision concerning the daily sacrifice, the rebellion that causes desolation, the surrender of the sanctuary and the trampling underfoot of the Lord's people?" (v. 13)

EXAMPLE

9:24–27: "seventy 'sevens' … seven 'sevens' … sixty-two 'sevens' … one 'seven.' In the middle of the 'seven' "

CONTEXT

Larger: Prayer of Penitence

Immediate: "while" (v. 20); "while" (v. 21); "As soon as you began to pray, a word went out" (v. 23); "Therefore, consider the word and understand the vision" (v. 23)

EXAMPLE

10:13–14: "But[25] the prince of the Persian kingdom resisted me twenty-one days" (v. 13); "for the vision concerns a time yet to come" (v. 14)

CONTEXT

"I have come in response to them" (v. 12); "now I have come to explain to you what will happen to your people in the future" (v. 14)

EXAMPLE

12:7: "It will be for a time, times and half a time"

CONTEXT

"How long will it be before these astonishing things are fulfilled?" (v. 6b); "I heard, but I did not understand, so I asked, 'My Lord, what will the outcome of all this be?' " (v. 8)

EXAMPLE
12:11: "From the time that the daily sacrifice is abolished and the abomination that causes desolation is set up, there will be 1,290 days"
CONTEXT
Larger: vv. 5–7
Immediate: 'I asked, "My Lord, what will be the outcome of all this be?"

EXAMPLE
12:12: "Blessed is the one who waits for and reaches the end of the 1,335 days"
CONTEXT
Larger: vv. 5–7
Immediate: Enclosed by "I heard, but I did not understand, so I asked, 'My Lord, what will be the outcome of all this be?' He replied, 'Go your way, Daniel, because the words are rolled up and sealed until the time of the end' " (vv. 8–9); "As for you, go your way till the end. You will rest, and then at the end of the days you will rise to receive your allotted inheritance" (v.13)

MOST
URGENT

As we can see from their context, the timetables provide the captive community comfort, encouragement, and strength to persevere as they anticipate God's intervention while facing an uncertain future. As we connect our world today with the world of the text, we see that we can boldly approach God in whatever context we find ourselves in. We may not receive a concrete answer to our question, "How much longer?" But we will be comforted, encouraged, and strengthened.

Conclusion

Walking down the path of a three-world approach, we looked at two key factors that are important in understanding Daniel's visions and connecting them to our own lives. The first is the use of first-person perspective, which invites all readers to experience the visions along with Daniel. Second, we have unpacked the visions' significance for the original readers. Even with the historical information available to us, there are still areas of profound mystery for us. However, time and again, the original audience was assured of the certainty of the events yet to come.

> We can boldly approach God in whatever context we find ourselves in, and we will be comforted, encouraged, and strengthened.

While in chapters 1-6, the sovereignty of God is firmly established as the central theme, the mystery of the end-time events overwhelms Daniel (7:28; 10:8-21). The two portions of the book—the court tales in chapters 1-6 and visions in chapters 7-12—blend together, underscoring the core message of the book: that those who believe may glimpse the mystery of the sovereign God.

☐   If you have time, read the whole of
     Daniel 7–12.

☐   Jeremiah 25:8–14

☐   Read the prayers of repentance in
     Daniel 9, Ezra 9, and Nehemiah 9, and
     compare them. What do they all have in
     common? How are they different?

Reflection

What impact does Daniel's first-person perspective
have on you as you read?

_____

_____

_____

How do you come to terms with the idea that God
reveals heavenly secrets to us yet at the same time
leaves us in suspense?

_____

_____

_____

THE APOCALYPTIC
GOD IN DANIEL

The book of Daniel shows us new dimensions of the Old Testament view of God. Especially the description of the apocalyptic God, which is important in Daniel but seldom discussed. As we continue to walk through the world of/within the text of Daniel, we'll build on our earlier discussions and look at other ways that the text depicts God. In this way, we will draw connections between the first half (court tales) and second half (visions) of the book.

First, the book as a whole uses a multitude of names, references, and elaborate descriptions to present us with a multifaceted view of the Hebrew God. In the court tales (chs. 1–6), the narrator has a sharp focus on the hand of God. God actively works among his faithful servants—Daniel and his three friends—through miraculous rescues, protection, and guidance. God is in control of the rising and falling of kings and empires, as well as in the promotion and survival of Daniel and his faithful group. From another angle, the sovereignty of God is exhibited through the contests between two kings—first Belshazzar, then Darius—and the confident Daniel (chs. 5 and 6), between the earthly rulers and the Hebrew God (ch. 3, esp. v. 29), and between court officials and Daniel (chs. 2–6). Reading the book as resistance literature or as a survival manual,[1] one can see the overarching message that the hand of God is always working in the history of Judah; it's a message that echoes through every chapter of the book.

With the view of God presented in the historical recitation of 9:2–19 (the penitential prayer) as a theological backbone, chapters 7–12 use a host of highly descriptive elements and a variety of names to present us with an otherworldly, awe-inspiring portrait of the sovereign God. God is the Ancient of Days; the one who carries out judgment (7:9–10) and sets the appointed time (11:27, 29, 33); the humanlike figure riding on clouds (7:13–14); the one who works through his angels and heavenly messengers, like Gabriel and Michael (7:21–27; 8:13–16; 10:12–11:1; 12:5–7); the Most Holy and the Anointed One (9:24–26). God is the one dressed in linen above the water of the river (12:5–6). The most extraordinary description is the luminous and fearful man (10:2–6) who speaks like the sound of a multitude (10:6). God is also the divine warrior who fights for his people and punishes those who oppress them (chs. 10–11).

To modern readers, not only is this portrayal of God rich and splendid, but it also engages our senses and imaginations through its use of "apocalyptic" literary traits to communicate its theology. A rational analysis of the names of God wouldn't be enough. Moreover, the apocalyptic understanding of God is revealed to us through the visions of Daniel, in his own voice. Daniel watches with his eyes, hears with his ears, feels the impact of the visions physically and emotionally, seeks to understand the full extent of the visions, and initiates the deep cry, "How long?" (12:6–8). Through the literary medium of a first-person vision report, Daniel invites all of his contemporaries, as well as we modern readers, into the experiential dimension of his visions. In other words, Daniel views God as a being who may be experienced in life-transforming ways by people of faith. Readers are encouraged to experience God as Daniel experiences him: with all our being, and in awe of him.

> Experience God as Daniel experiences him: with all your being, and in awe of him.

APOCALYPTIC LITERATURE

The word "apocalypse" derives from the Greek word for a supernatural revelation (*apokalypsis*). Revelations in the Bible are usually visions, which are explained by an angel, concerning heavenly mysteries (for instance, God's throne in heaven or the climax of history). Some of the imagery in Daniel's visions parallel ancient Near Eastern mythology (for example, beasts rising from the sea, the figure riding on the clouds, etc.). There are also parallels to earlier passages in the Hebrew Bible (see Isa 24–27).[2]

Second, the distinctiveness of the portrayal of God within the book of Daniel is shown in the extent of God's intervention. In the Old Testament, God is reaching out and speaking to humanity through the voice of Moses and the prophets.[3] Psalms, Proverbs, Ecclesiastes, and Job show us a new side of the dynamic: humanity is reaching out/speaking to God. The realm of this twofold framework (God reaching out/speaking to humanity and humanity reaching out/speaking to God) is placed *within* the history of humankind—in other words, on the earthly scene. In Daniel, from chapter 11 onward, God's intervention in the history of humankind is slowly moving toward another sphere—over and beyond human history.

This is the true function of apocalyptic literature: It takes an entirely new genre to communicate the mystery of the sovereign God, the events of the end times, and the dynamics in their unfolding, such as the final victory of God for his people (11:40–12:10), the promise of resurrected life (12:2–3, 12), and the eternal perseverance of the people of God (the saints; 12:11–12). God's intervention moves from the earthly scene to a realm of over and beyond human history.

Third, the book of Daniel portrays God as mysterious. There are dimensions of the apocalyptic vision of God that are puzzling to Daniel—not to mention to us modern readers—even when angels explain his vision. Perhaps this fits with the function and nature of apocalyptic literature—to communicate mysteries while maintaining their mysteriousness. It would be difficult for us to pinpoint all of the characteristics of God shown in Daniel. Among the emphatic announcements that the visions are true (10:1), and that the message is truth from the Book

> He is the one who decrees, who sets appointed times, and who is in full control of world events.

of Truth (11:2), and in the assurance that things will happen at the appointed time, readers may acquire glimpses into the mystery of the sovereign God.[4] He is the one who decrees, who sets appointed times, and who is in full control of world events.

SUGGESTED READING

☐　Read Isaiah 24–27, and look for any similar phrases or images in Daniel 7–12.

☐　Read the depiction of Jesus in Revelation 1:9–20, looking for similar phrases to those used in Daniel 7–12. Why do you think John chose these phrases as he was writing?

Reflection

Chapter 9 presents to us a multifaceted view of God through the history of Israel. Reflect on your experiential knowledge of God as your redeemer, covenant-maker, and sovereign.

_____

_____

_____

_____

_____

Have you ever acknowledged that the God of your life here-and-now is also an apocalyptic God? If God's intervention extends over and beyond human history, how would this knowledge and affirmation affect the way you live your life now?

_____

_____

_____

5

DANIEL AND OUR OWN TRANSFORMATION

Kazoh Kitamori was probably the first Asian-American theologian to contribute to the theology of the pain of God. His monograph *Theology of the Pain of God*[1] came out in the mid-1960s. In identifying himself with the pain and suffering of the Japanese nation during the aftermath of the atomic bomb, he wrote this insightful and penetrating book. As a young seminarian reading his book in the 1970s, I was astonished by the depth of his insight as well as by his level of engagement in the subject. Kitamori relives the national suffering and shame and reexpresses such emotional pain that I was deeply moved by reading about his experience. In the context of biblical interpretation, this process may be referred to as the process of "appropriation," in which the experiences of others in an ancient text—in our case, the book of Daniel—are brought into conversation with modern faith.

Appropriation

We begin with the concept of appropriation as the practice of bringing any given text in the Bible into contextual relevance for the reader. Andrew D. Kille notes that "appropriation involves not only an analysis of various aspects of the text, it requires a *reexpression* of those elements in a way the reader can grasp."[2] Appropriation is a two-way street, from the world of the text to the circumstances of the reader and vice versa. It takes place in the interactive space between the reader's own world and the possible world projected by the text and is controlled neither by the text nor by the reader. Appropriation occurs in the intersection between text and reader, through the interplay of their perspectives, and takes two distinct steps: *reliving* and *reexpressing.*

THE EMOTIVE REALM

There is a famous Chinese saying regarding the art of reading poetry and appreciating a painting—*shi qing hua yi*—which literally means "the *emotive* realm of Chinese poetry and painting." This emotive realm is the locus of appreciation, as well as understanding. As readers engage in the visionary experience of Daniel, the emotions that chapters 7–12 convey and elicit capture multiple dimensions of our perception and thus shape our understanding of the text's message.

Toward a Renewed Affirmation of Our Faith in the Apocalyptic God

We have already discussed the importance of the exotic and elaborate depictions of God in the book of Daniel, which are highlighted by a host of divine names. There is, however, always an element of mystery and suspense behind these depictions. Just like the exilic community in Daniel's time, our collective and individual experiences of God are most often based on who God is.

God saves, protects, guides, comforts, sustains, and empowers us through his intervention in our lives. Through the six court tales (chs. 1–6), the original audience learned of and preserved the acts of God as they played out in history. In a similar way, our faith is built on the promises and our experiential knowledge of God. The revelation of various dimensions of divine mystery, especially toward the end of the present era (chs. 11 and 12), creates a sense of suspense and uncertainty that may challenge our faith. Daniel expresses the same sentiment with his earnest desire to know "how long?" (12:6). The same inquiry, "How long will it take for the vision to be fulfilled?" (8:13), in combination with nonspecific references (for example, "at the appointed time" [11:27, 29]; "a time yet to come" [10:14]) and the timeframe presented via the apocalyptic timetables[3] (for example, 2,300 evenings and

> God saves, protects, guides, comforts, sustains, and empowers us through his intervention in our lives.

mornings [8:14]; 1,290 days and 1,335 days [12:12]) suggest that our interpretive goal should not be to decode the mysteries of Daniel but to renew our faith in the Most High and sovereign God, the God of gods (11:36). The narrator drives this point home most strongly at the end of the four visions. Toward the end of the first-person retellings of the visions, Daniel is given a promissory charge: "But you, go on to the end, and you shall rest and stand in your lot at the end of days" (12:13, my translation).

On the one hand, we may wonder whether it is enough for Daniel to "go on to the end," whenever that may be, or if more is required of him. The same could be said of the ideas of "rest" and "[rising] to receive your allotted inheritance" (12:13). On the other hand, the promise of resurrection and eternal reward was more distant and foreign for Daniel and his contemporaries than for us. The ending of Daniel is, in essence, a call to put our trust in the eternal promise of the sovereign God who will bring these things to pass at their appointed time. At the end of Daniel's visionary experience, that which has calmed his tormented soul also has a soothing effect on us: "But you, [Carver/Christine/Warren], go on to the end; for you shall rest and stand in your lot at the end of days" (12:13, my translation).

Second, in addition to the revelation of God through the other books of the Old Testament, God's intervention in the book of Daniel is over and beyond human history (especially in chs. 11–12). From the third-person perspective of the narrator of chapters 1–6, God's sovereignty manifests through his work on the earthly scene. God continues to rule over world events in present and future eras, and will be in control over and beyond human history.

What, then, are the implications for those of us who are pilgrims on this journey? To relive the turbulence of Daniel's time and to reexpress the significance of this aspect of the apocalyptic God so that, somehow, we can come to terms with the extent of human evil and the intensity and magnitude of human suffering in our chaotic world. In spite of current appearances, the sovereign God is still in control—this is how we may appropriate the message of Daniel in our daily lives.

> In spite of current appearances, the sovereign God is still in control.

Daniel as Resistance Literature and as a Survival Manual[4]

Reading Daniel chapters 1–6 as resistance literature and as a manual for survival highlights the coping strategy that Daniel adopts. Daniel's world is unpleasant and difficult for him because he is a religious and ethnic minority under foreign rule. Perseverance and the ability to adapt are necessary tools for survival. If we read Daniel as a success story, the overall values of the narrator of chapters 1–6 are loyalty, optimism, and, perhaps, accommodation to the ruling power, but not to the extent of giving up individual identity (in Daniel's case, being a Jew from Judea). Crossing borders between their home and host cultures, immigrant families today go through the same journey of alienation, adaptation, assimilation, and, for some, reorientation. As in Daniel, pleasure, pain, success, and failure are among the possibilities of border crossing. Daniel exemplifies an individual's breaking away from captive status to become an aspiring sage in an adopted culture, bringing the positive characteristics provided to him by his home culture into the royal court and using his background for the good of all. Failing to see this possibility, we might remain perpetual captives in a free land, hiding the good that we have to offer our new situation and neighbors.

Daniel is also a text that is often appropriated by people who discover that it speaks to the contexts in which they find themselves. In 9:2, Daniel himself turns to a text—Jeremiah—as he seeks to understand his present situation. In doing so, he mirrors our search for meaning and significance in the traditions that have been handed down to us. If Daniel can be read as a manual for survival under hostile and dominating empires,[5] then Daniel and his group's coping strategy is the subtle yet creative use of satire and humor. This may have profound implications for coping strategies on the part of minority persons today—in society at large, as well as in some professional fields.

The "Daniel" in Each of Us: Tension between Public and Private

No characterization of Daniel would be complete without attending to the fact that the book presents us with two Daniels: the public Daniel as portrayed in the court tales of chapters 1–6, and the private Daniel in the first-person reports of chapters 7–12. Daniel's public self is the epitome of self-confidence—an aspiring sage. He climbs the "corporate ladder," from a captive prisoner to the prime minister of the whole kingdom (6:28). The summary appraisal in 6:28 best captures the accomplishments of the public Daniel: "So Daniel prospered during the reign of Darius and the reign of Cyrus the Persian." Time and again, Daniel is described as a man with the spirit of the holy gods and possessing superior qualities that stand out, distinct among his peers.

As discussed already, the twelve chapters of Daniel are not arranged in chronological order. The visions in chapters 7 and 8 occur during the reign of King Belshazzar of Babylon, presumably before the events in chapter 5. Chapters 6 and 9 take place during the reign of Darius. The last vision (chapters 10–12) occurs during the reign of Cyrus. An arrangement of the chronology of the chapters has important bearing on Daniel, as his public and private personas are simultaneously revealed to us within the same temporal timeframe. If we were to read the chapters in chronological order, rather than how they are arranged currently, we would find that while Daniel functions publicly as an aspiring sage with insight, intelligence, and outstanding wisdom to interpret dreams (5:12, 14), he simultaneously admits that the vision is beyond his understanding (8:27). Deeply troubled (7:15, 28) and exhausted by his visions, he lies ill for several days. Yet he still has to get up and attend to his public functions—the king's business (8:27). In his private life, he has to keep troubling thoughts and matters to himself (7:28). Another sharp contrast prevails as we compare Daniel's two selves. In chapter 5, a bold, self-confident Daniel confronts a weak and frightened Belshazzar. Yet in his private life, Daniel's fear is described in much the same manner as the king's (compare 7:15, 28; 8:17, 27 with 5:6, 9–10).

A closer look at the inner conflict of Daniel suggests a certain tension caused by his ability to interpret the dreams of others and the difficulty he experiences in interpreting his own visions. Daniel's ability to understand visions and dreams of all kinds is a gift from God (1:17), and he thus distinguishes himself among the administrators and satraps by these exceptional qualities (6:3). Living through his own visionary experience places Daniel in a predicament as both an outstanding sage and an overwhelmed, troubled seer. This tension may contribute to the emotional upheaval and symptoms of physical illness that the private Daniel suffers.

From a pastoral perspective, the effect of the inner life of Daniel on the corporate dimension—the community of saints—is seldom focused on. We potentially have a "Daniel" in each of us and in each of our communities. Yes, the world of Daniel is full of conflict, turbulence, and the rising and falling of kings and empires. It is also a world that the book of Daniel may express only through imagery, embedded in dreams and visions. Yet, as we penetrate the surface of the text and zoom in to those deeper structures below, we are drawn to the internal world of Daniel—his private self. In other words, as Daniel engages our feelings through his first-person descriptions, we may naturally bypass the turbulent external world of Daniel and touch his inner feelings through our engagement with the text. In my case, my reading takes me from Daniel's public self as an aspiring sage to my public role as a theological educator and shepherd-teacher; from his private self as a suffering seer to aspects of my own inner life.

In short, Daniel's interior world is a world of paradoxes. Daniel asks but cannot comprehend the answer; he wants to know but fails to understand; he sees but cannot perceive; he hears but is unable to respond. As we seek to interact with both Daniels, public and private, and as we relive and reexpress Daniel's conflicting emotions and appropriate them to our own context, we may find that we face the same dilemma in some areas of our lives. We may shine light on areas where we cannot meet our own expectations or understand what we wish to understand. What this parallel between us and Daniel teaches is that sometimes we must rely not on our own abilities but on the certainty of God's "vision," his timing, and the promise of things eternal.

> We must rely not on our own abilities but on the certainty of God's "vision," his timing, and the promise of things eternal.

Daniel's Probing Spirit and the Path to Transformation

As discussed in the above section, Daniel's external world is that of peril and turbulence, while his interior world is full of paradox. In chapters 7–12, even with the aid of angelic explanation, Daniel admits that the meanings of the visions are beyond his understanding. Given that the interpretation of some parts of the visions is meant to remain sealed forever (8:26; 12:4), the probing spirit of Daniel provides us with pointers toward the path of transformation.

All through his first-person vision reports, one thing truly captures our attention: Daniel never ceases to ask for a fuller understanding of the meaning or fulfillment of the visions. His inquiring spirit is evident: "Then I wanted to know the meaning" (7:19); "I heard, but I did not understand. So I asked" (12:8); "While I, Daniel, was watching the vision and trying to understand it" (8:15). Daniel also initiates the question "How long?" (12:6). Instead of getting a concrete answer, he is assured that the fulfillment of the vision is certain and will be realized at "the time of the end" (8:17); "at the appointed time" (11:24, 29); and that the message is true (10:1) and concerns the Book of Truth (10:21).

To contemporary readers, Daniel's inquiring spirit may be regarded as a key directive toward the path of "faith seeking understanding." Though faced with bewilderment, frustration, and puzzling thoughts time and again, Daniel is assured and reassured of the promise of the sovereign God—everything will happen *at the appointed time*. In like manner, embracing our lives along with all of life's trials, we have been in the same situation—spiritually and physically asking God "How long?" Readers are encouraged to seek a deeper level of experiential understanding of what is happening and has happened in our lives and in the lives of the people around us. With faith as our basis, we may seek to understand and experience more and more of God's sovereignty and mystery. To appropriate Daniel's probing spirit into our faith journey is to be invigorated, and it may well be the function of the first-person perspective of the vision reports. This is another example of how we may reexpress what we learn from Daniel, the person, in our own attempt to improve our understanding of God through engagement with Daniel, the book.

SUGGESTED READING

- ☐ Reread Daniel 1, focusing on what it would feel like to be Daniel, surviving in and resisting an unfamiliar culture.
- ☐ Reread Daniel 12:8–13, noting Daniel's probing spirit and the response to that probing spirit.

Reflection

What is required of us to "relive" and "reexpress" every time we seek to appropriate biblical truth?

_____

_____

_____

Do you agree with the fact that we all have a "Daniel" inside us—experiencing the same disjunction between public expectation and our own life experience? If so, how can the book of Daniel provide us with an example of how to live with this tension?

_____

_____

_____

6

CONCLUSION

Daniel is a difficult book. Decoding the apocalyptic timetables and demystifying the exotic dreams and visions to a full extent are both beyond our reach. We lack the tools necessary to gain a firm grip on the meaning and specifics of Daniel's visions. However, as many have rightly noted, it is the function of apocalyptic literature to unveil end-time mysteries, but to do so in a way that conceals these mysteries from those who are not meant to understand. Assigning a sixth-century date for the book places most, if not all, of the events to come in the "near" and "distant" future for the first audience. In other words, the key to uncovering the significance of the book of Daniel, for both the original audience and readers of today, is to engage the question of how to handle the element of mystery in our faith.

The book of Daniel does not provide us with the "how," but it does provide us glimpses into the mystery of the sovereign God. Time and again, we are assured of the certainty and truth of the events yet to come. The book's twelve chapters allow us to perceive the same hand of God working in human history, and also over and beyond the present human era. Through the inquiring spirit of Daniel, we are reminded of our limits to fully comprehend but are encouraged to embark on a journey of faith that is fueled by the quest for understanding. The notion of mystery and suspense, and the awareness that only glimpses of the mystery of God are available to us, create an inviting space for all readers to engage and to appropriate the collective message of Daniel. It is in this area of appropriation that this mysterious and puzzling book may become so meaningful.

The book of Daniel, like all biblical books, is read by people of many diverse cultures and contexts. A North American reader, a Christian from Korea, or a refugee from Syria, each in their own way, would come up with a collection of diverse, ever-enriching, and meaning-expanding readings. With full awareness of my social and cultural location in North America, and knowing that my reading could in no way be considered representative of the Chinese-Canadian perspective, I shall take a cue from Daniel and use my first-person perspective to conclude this book with a self-engaged version of appropriation in its two steps: reliving and reexpressing.

Reliving: I used to swim ten laps daily at the YMCA near my home. Earlier this year, I lost three friends to cancer, all within a period of six weeks. Instead of counting the laps, it has become my habit to pray for one person in

> A North American reader, a Christian from Korea, or a refugee from Syria, each in their own way, would come up with a collection of diverse, ever-enriching, and meaning-expanding readings of the book of Daniel.

need during each lap of my swim. The first time, when I was at the pool after attending the third funeral, the harsh reminder of the reality of losing everyone I had prayed for struck me really hard.

Reexpressing: Months later, I was still overwhelmed by the feeling of sadness and loss, to the extent that what Daniel said in Daniel 10:16–17—"I am overcome with anguish because of the vision, my Lord, and I feel very weak. How can I, your servant, talk with you, my Lord? My strength is gone and I can hardly breathe"—had become my *felt* emotion. In spite of the spiritual and emotional condition that I was in, just like Daniel, I still had to get up and attend to my King's business (8:27): teaching and serving in various ministry capacities. Many times in my distress, I have come before the Lord and have experienced uplifting moments when God spoke to me, "Peace! Be strong now; be strong"—and I was strengthened (10:19).

Perhaps this is in no way regarded as an isolated experience in our lives and in the lives of the people around us. It is possible that I might experience the same kind of helpless and disheartening situation again later on in my life. I may have to go through the same scenario, and I will be strengthened time and again as I approach God for comfort and the strength to persevere.

As we contemplate the conclusion of Daniel (12:12–13), we might anticipate a more powerful, climactic, and dramatic ending after Daniel's exotic visionary experience, especially after the fourth vision. Reading 12:12 as a blessing and encouragement for those who persevere, we can see that verses 12–13 together are an empowering ending, though oftentimes we ask, "Is that enough, Lord?" I invite all readers to reflect silently and deeply on this promissory charge of God: "But you, [Pastor Grace/Brother Tony/Sister Gladys], go on to the end; for you shall rest and stand in your lot at the end of the days" (12:13, my translation). It is a serene but assuring hope.

SELECTED
BIBLIOGRAPHY

Baldwin, Joyce G. *Daniel*. Tyndale Old Testament Commentaries. Leicester: Inter-Varsity Press, 1978.

———. "Theology of Daniel." In *New International Dictionary of Old Testament Theology and Exegesis (NIDOTTE)*, edited by Willem A. VanGemeren, 4:499. 5 vols. Grand Rapids: Zondervan, 1997.

Collins, John. *Daniel: With an Introduction to Apocalyptic Literature*. Forms of Old Testament Literature. Grand Rapids: Eerdmans, 1984.

Coogan, Michael David. *The Old Testament: A Historical and Literary Introduction to the Hebrew Scriptures*. New York: Oxford University Press, 2006.

Fewell, D. N. *Circle of Sovereignty: Plotting Politics in the Book of Daniel*. Nashville: Abingdon, 1991.

Fokkelman, J. P. *Reading Biblical Narrative: An Introductory Guide*. Translated by Ineke Smit. Louisville, KY: Westminster John Knox, 1999.

Goldingay, John E. *Daniel*. Word Biblical Commentary. Dallas: Word, 1987.

Gurney, R. J. M. "The Seventy Weeks of Daniel 9:24–27." *Evangelical Quarterly* 53 (1981): 29–36.

Hartman, Lars. "The Function of Some So-called Apocalyptic Timetables." *New Testament Studies* 22 (1976): 1–14.

Hewitt, C. M. K. "Guidelines to the Interpretation of Daniel and Revelation." In *A Guide to Biblical*

Prophecy, edited by C. E. Armerding and W. W. Gasque, 101–16. 2nd ed. Peabody, MA: Hendrickson, 1989.

Kille, D. Andrew. *Psychological Biblical Criticism*. Minneapolis: Fortress, 2001.

Kirkpatrick, Shane. *Competing for Honor: A Social-Scientific Reading of Daniel 1–6*. BIS74. Leiden: Brill, 2005.

Kitamori, Kazoh. *Theology of the Pain of God*. London: SCM Press, 1966.

Leung Lai, Barbara M. "Aspirant Sage or Dysfunctional Seer? Cognitive Dissonance and Pastoral Vulnerability in the Profile of Daniel." *Pastoral Psychology* 57 (2008): 199–210.

———. "Daniel." In *The People's Bible: New Revised Standard Version*, edited by Curtis Paul DeYoung, Wilda C. Gafney, Leticia Guardiola-Sáenz, George E. Tinker, and Frank Yamada, 1014–15. Philadelphia: Fortress Press, 2008.

———. *Through the "I"-Window: The Inner Life of Characters in the Hebrew Bible*. Hebrew Bible Monographs 34. Sheffield: Sheffield Phoenix Press, 2011.

———. "Word Becoming Flesh [On Appropriation]: Engaging Daniel as a Survival Manual." In *Global Voices: Reading the Bible in the Majority World*, edited by Craig S. Keener and M. Daniel Carroll R., chapter 5. Peabody, MA: Hendrickson, 2012.

Longman, Tremper III. *Daniel*. NIV Application Commentary. Grand Rapids: Zondervan, 1999.

Lucas, E. C. "The Origin of Daniel's Four Empires Scheme Re-examined." *Tyndale Bulletin* 40: (1989): 185–202.

Niskanen, Paul. "Daniel's Portrait of Antiochus IV: Echoes of a Persian King." *Catholic Biblical Quarterly* 66 (2004): 378–86.

Redditt, Paul L. "The Community behind the Book of Daniel: Challenges, Hopes, Values, and Its View of God." *Perspectives in Religious Studies* 36 (2009): 321–39.

Russell, David S. "Apocalyptic Imagery as Political Cartoon?" In *After the Exile: Essays in Honour of Rex Mason*, edited by John Barton and David J. Reimer, 191–200. Macon: Mercer University Press, 1996.

———. *Daniel, An Active Volcano: Reflection on the Book of Daniel.* Louisville: Westminster John Knox, 1989.

Tate, W. Randolph. *Biblical Interpretation: An Integrated Approach.* 3rd ed. Peabody, MA: Hendrickson, 2008.

Valeta, David M. *Lions and Ovens and Visions: A Satirical Reading of Daniel 1–6.* HBM 12. Sheffield: Sheffield Phoenix, 2008.

Wallace, Ronald S. *The Message of Daniel.* Bible Speaks Today. Downers Grove, IL: InterVarsity Press, 1979.

Wenham, D. "The Kingdom of God and Daniel." *Expository Times* 98 (1987): 132–34.

Woodard, B. L., Jr. "Literary Strategies and Authorship in the Book of Daniel." *Journal of the Evangelical Theological Society* 37 (1994): 39–53.

Wong, G. C. I. "Faithful to the End: A Pastoral Reading of Daniel 10–12." *Expository Times* 110 (1999): 109–13.

NOTES

Chapter 1: Introduction

1. Tremper Longman III, *Daniel,* NIV Application Commentary (Grand Rapids: Zondervan, 1999), 13.

2. See Barbara Leung Lai, "Word Becoming Flesh [On Appropriation]: Engaging Daniel as a Survival Manual," in *Global Voices: Reading the Bible in the Majority World*, ed. Craig S. Keener and M. Daniel Carroll R. (Peabody, MA: Hendrickson, 2012), chapter 5.

3. Longman, Daniel, 26

4. Except in the case of chapter 4.

5. Note that the same reading strategy has been recommended by John Goldingay, *Daniel*, Word Biblical Commentary (Dallas: Word, 1987), xl.

6. For the reason behind the shift from Hebrew to Aramaic to Hebrew, see the discussion in Anathea E. Portier-Young, "Language of Identity of Obligation: Daniel as Bilingual Book," *Vetus Testamentum* 60 (2010): 98–115.

7. Among evangelical biblical scholars, there is no common consensus regarding the dating of Daniel. John Goldingay interprets the book as finally redacted in the second century BC (see Goldingay, *Daniel*, xl). He notes also that "whether the stories are history or fiction, the visions actual prophecy or quasi-prophecy [i.e., prophecy written after the events], written by Daniel or someone else, in the sixth century B. C., the second, or somewhere in between, makes surprisingly little difference to the book's exegesis" (xl). Similarly, Joyce Baldwin notes, "The fact that the standpoint of the writer (sixth or second century BC) cannot be ascertained for certain does not greatly affect the interpretation" (Joyce Baldwin, "Theology of Daniel," *New International Dictionary of Old Testament Theology and Exegesis [NIDOTTE]*, 4:499.) See also Longman's argument for a sixth century date of the book in *Daniel*, 21–24.

8. See a classic but helpful discussion, C. M. Kempton Hewitt, "Guidelines to the Interpretation of Daniel and Revelation," in *A Guide to Biblical Prophecy*, ed. Carl E. Armerding and W. Ward Gasque (Grand Rapids: Baker, 1997), 101–16.

Chapter 2: The Sovereignty of God on the Earthly Scene

1. On this see J. P. Fokkelman, *Reading Biblical Narrative: An Introductory Guide* (trans. Ineke Smit) Louisville: Westminster John Knox, 1999), esp. ch. 2.

2. See Danna Nolan Fewell, *Circle of Sovereignty: Plotting Politics in the Book of Daniel* (Nashville: Abingdon, 1991).

3. Shane Kirkpatrick, *Competing for Honor: A Social-Scientific Reading of Daniel 1–6* BIS74; (Leiden: Brill, 2005).

4. See David M. Valeta, *Lions and Ovens and Visions: Satirical Reading of Daniel 1–6* HBM 12; (Sheffield: Sheffield Phoenix Press, 2008).

5. David S. Russell, "Apocalyptic Imagery as Political Cartoon?," in *After the Exile: Essays in Honour of Rex Mason* ed. John Barton and David J. Reimer; (Macon: Mercer University Press, 1996), 192–99.

6. Hewitt, "Guidelines," 105.

7. As part of the requirements for the so-called "three-year passage to the Babylonian court" (v. 5b).

8. The same Hebrew word is used here in both v. 7 (fixed/set) and v. 8 (laid on).

9. From John D. Barry et al., *Faithlife Study Bible* (Bellingham, WA: Lexham Press, 2012, 2016), Dan 1:7.

10. For more information on how multivocality works in Hebrew literature, see Francis Landy, "Vision and Voice in Isaiah," *Journal for the Study of the Old Testament* 88 (2000):19–36.

11. Note that the instruments are listed in the same order in vv. 5a, 7a, 10a, and 15a.

12. Longman, *Daniel*, 117.

13. According to ancient texts and archaeological discoveries, the Babylonian Empire at Nebuchadnezzar's time was indeed at its prime, and its boundary was grand. See Longman, *Daniel*, 121, especially n. 14.

14. According to Babylonian records, Belshazzar was not a direct descendant of Nebuchadnezzar, who died in 562 BC. Nabonidus is recorded as the last king of Babylon (556–539 BC). Belshazzar was actually the son of Nabonidus and was put in charge of Babylon during the years that his father was away from the capital city. The exact dates of Belshazzar's coregency are not known. For a more detailed discussion, see Goldingay, *Daniel*, 106–8.

15. The same Hebrew word is used in both places.

16. Verse 6 in the Hebrew Bible; this is a literal translation.

17. Adapted in part from *Faithlife Study Bible*, Dan 5:25.

18. Verse 26 in the Hebrew Bible.

19. Compare the inclusiveness of the use of "all" and "every" in the decree in chapter 3—here is a reversal, the call for *all* peoples to fear and revere the God of Daniel.

Chapter 3: From the Earthly to the Heavenly Realm

1. The same movement has been observed by Longman, *Daniel*, 177.

2. As Goldingay has commented, "The best approach [to the study of Daniel] is to take him on his own terms and immerse ourselves in the visionary experience as he describes it" (Goldingay, *Daniel*, xl).

3. That is, the timetables concerning the unfolding of future events from the perspective of a sixth-century BC textual background.

4. C. M. K. Hewitt, "Guidelines to the Interpretation of Daniel and Revelation," *A Guide to Biblical Prophecy*, 102.

5. Michael David Coogan, *The Old Testament: A Historical and Literary Introduction to the Hebrew Scriptures* (New York: Oxford University Press, 2006).

6. D. A. Neal, "Apocalyptic Literature, Introduction to," in *The Lexham Bible Dictionary*, ed. John D. Barry et al. (Bellingham, WA: Lexham Press, 2016); Coogan, *The Old Testament*, 436.

7. W. Randolph Tate is one of the first scholars to introduce and promote this three-world approach to biblical interpretation. See Tate, *Biblical Interpretation: An Integrated Approach*, 3rd ed. (Peabody, MA: Hendrickson, 2008), 1–10. See also Corrine

L. Carvalho, *Primer on Biblical Methods* (Winona, MN: Anselm Academic, 2009).

8. It is not necessary to read into the text the New Testament connotation of the "Son of Man" here, although the Gospel writers (compare Acts 7:56) and the author of Revelation (Rev 1:13; 14:14) certainly adopt Daniel's use of the phrase and apply it to Jesus Christ to express his dual nature as both human and divine, capable of approaching the throne of God and given majesty, power, glory, and followers of all backgrounds. Literally, the Hebrew text of Daniel 7:13 means "one who looks like a human being" or "a humanlike figure" (compare Num 23:19; Ezek 2–3). See Goldingay, *Daniel*, 168–72.

9. I will provide a recommendation to the interpretation of the apocalyptic timetables (periods, numbers, and days) at the end of this chapter.

10. For discussion on the identification of the fourth beast as Greece and the climactic horn (v. 21) as Antiochus IV, see Goldingay, *Daniel*, 179–82; Longman, *Daniel*, 188–91. For more on Antiochus IV Epiphanes, see H. Daniel Zacharias, "Antiochus IV Epiphanes," in *The Lexham Bible Dictionary*, ed. John D. Barry et al. (Bellingham, WA: Lexham Press, 2016).

11. This may refer to the angelic beings (see Longman, *Daniel*, 188).

12. Goldingay, *Daniel*, 182.

13. Daily life, according to Old Testament tradition, is not reckoned on the basis of a twenty-four-hour time period. As Simon DeVries observes, this distinctive time concept gives definition and quality to one's existence. Time is perceived as an experience-filled, meaningful continuum. See Simon John DeVries, *Yesterday, Today and Tomorrow: Time and History in the Old Testament* (Grand Rapids: Eerdmans, 1975), 31. See also the discussion on the Hebrew concept of time in Barbara Leung Lai, "Making Sense of the Biblical Portrait: Toward an Interpretive Strategy for the 'Virtuous Wife' in Proverbs 31:10–31," *Teach Me Your Paths: Studies in Old Testament Theology and Literature*, ed. John Kessler and Jeffrey P. Greenman (Toronto: Clements, 2001), 77–78.

14. See Longman, *Daniel*, 210–15, on "numbers in apocalyptic literature" and "misuses of apocalyptic." I will propose a con-

textual approach to the interpretation of the apocalyptic timetables after our discussion of the last vision (Dan 10–12).

15. They divided the empire for ease of rule. See John Collins, *Daniel: with an Introduction to Apocalyptic Literature,* Forms of Old Testament Literature (Grand Rapids: Eerdmans, 1984), 87–88; and Joyce G. Baldwin, *Daniel* (Leicester: IVP, 1978), 158–62.

16. See 90n10.

17. I follow the same as outlined in Longman, *Daniel*, 226.

18. In Hebrew, the conjunction *waw* could suggest a progression here between (1) and (2).

19. Longman, *Daniel*, 225–228.

20. Baldwin, *Daniel,* 173.

21. Unless we take the vision in chapter 11 as recorded after its fulfillment. Compare the view taken by Goldingay, *Daniel*, 282–83.

22. See Leung Lai, *Through the "I"-Window*, 20–21.

23. In my reading of the four visions, I have intentionally set aside the discussion of the numbers and the calculation of times in the apocalyptic timetables in Daniel. Instead of attending to methods of decoding the dates and numbers, Lars Hartman has long proposed a functional approach to their interpretation in "The Function of Some So-called Apocalyptic Timetables," *New Testament Studies* 22 (1976): 1–14. The discussion below is my response, providing an add-on contextual dimension to Hartman's. Rooted in the immediate textual context of the timetables within the four visions, the recommended approach can be referred to as a "functional-contextual" approach.

24. Similarly, Longman III states that the function of the highly symbolic numbers is "not for date-setting but for comfort" (*Daniel*, 215).

25. In Hebrew, "*waw* of contrast" (in the sense of "but") instead of "*waw* consecutive" (in the sense of "and").

Chapter 4: The Apocalyptic God in Daniel

1. This will be discussed with demonstrated examples in chapter 6 of this book.

2. Adapted from "Apocalyptic Literature," by John J. Collins, in John D. Barry, et al., *Faithlife Study Bible* (Bellingham, WA: Lexham Press, 2012, 2016).

3. The Hebrew Old Testament divides into three parts: Law, Prophets, and Writings. Law and Prophets are considered to be the first and second divisions of the Hebrew Bible. The book of Daniel, apocalyptic literature, is in the third division, the Writings.

4. This is a reminder that Daniel's visions can be understood up to a certain extent but not in full detail. The visions leave us uncertain about specifics but clearly affirm to us that the sovereign God is in control.

Chapter 5: Daniel and Our Own Transformation

1. Kazoh Kitamori, *Theology of the Pain of God* (Richmond: John Knox, 1965).

2. D. Andrew Kille, *Psychological Biblical Criticism* (Minneapolis: Fortress, 2001), 53; italics mine.

3. Compare discussion in chapter 4.

4. See Leung Lai, "Word Becoming Flesh," 65-77.

5. As advocated by Valeta; see chapter 3.